Seven Boxes

AN INSPIRATIONAL MEMOIR

Celebrating the Strength to Move On

BOBBI ALBA, ED.D.

credo
house publishers

Published in the United States by Credo House Publishers,
a division of Credo Communications LLC, Grand Rapids, Michigan
credohousepublishers.com

All Scripture quotations, unless otherwise indicated, are from The Holy Bible,
New International Version®, NIV.® Copyright © 1973, 1978, 1984, 2011 by Biblica, Inc.®
Used by permission. All rights reserved worldwide.

ISBN: 978-1-62586-141-2

Cover and interior design by Klaas Wolterstorff
Editing by Donna Huisjen

Printed in the United States of America
First edition

For my husband, Aurelio,

for his unwavering support in all areas of life.

For my transgender son who helped me be a transparent Mom.

For Jean, Paul, Mom, Dad, Zoe, and Zorro:

Thank you for sharing your journey with me.

TO PureFlix -
Thank you for
helping others find the
Strength to move on! Your
movies inspired me to write this
book + God willing share it with others
in a movie version (highlighting Big Daddy
Weave's song "My story". Please see Page vii.
This is my story, and it tells of Him!
Enjoy!

PS I was mentioned by
Dr. John Trent,
author. Scottsdale,
AZ.

Contents

Preface

On August 28, 2017, I experienced a moment like I have never be-fore. While I was drinking my morning tea, I sensed the Holy Spirit telling me to take notes because I was to write a book, and then flowed out a full outline. I could not write fast enough, and after the outline was written a few minutes later, I cried uncontrollably. I am not typically a crier, so this caught me off guard as it was from the very depths of my being. I was not a writer, I did not want to be an author of this genre, but I felt compelled to follow what I consider God's prompting upon my heart. My dad had recently died, and my dog had died a few days prior; I wasn't in the mindset for such an overwhelming task. However, I persevered and I present to you this labor of love. It is what I scribed in attempt to follow the calling set before me. I realized during this process that contemporary Christian singer Big Daddy Weave is spot on in his song about Jesus, "My Story." What you hold in your hands is *my* story, and it tells of *Him.* May you be blessed by *Seven Boxes: An Inspirational Memoir Celebrating the Strength to Move On.* I would love to hear from you about how this book has affected you. May you enjoy the journey!

Introduction

Hi friend! So good to see you! You found the place! I'd give you a hug, but I am dusty from cleaning. I really appreciate you being here. No worries, though; I will do the heavy lifting in more ways than one. Today I don't need physical help as much as emotional support. I just need someone to sit with me and keep me company on this journey, and I really wanted it to be you.

I know we don't really know each other very well yet. I was hoping we could get to know each other better by spending some quality bonding time together just talking and sharing. I need to finish this project today. I can't afford to keep my storage unit anymore. It is over $200 a month, but really, I am clearing it out not just for financial reasons but therapeutic reasons as well. Not only is there a physical cost of keeping things in storage, but an emotional cost.

So, come with me and let's get started! Down this dark, cement, musty hallway is my unit on the end. I have never seen another tenant here before, which is odd as I have had this unit for so many years. It is almost eerie, this building filled with ghosts of people's pasts. Don't get freaked out when you hear a loud metal door slam and everything in the hallway go black; it is just the exterior door closing since it is on a short timer. I love the jazz music from the local university radio station playing softly from overhead. It is kind of a mellow soundtrack to keep me company.

Here we are. I have already started clearing out the large items like my old microwave, so the unit's metal door is already opened. It is surprisingly clean since I haven't visited here in a while. I am just relieved that there are no spiders to be seen. The light bulb is still warming up to full glow. I hope you brought a jacket as the thick, gray cement blocks keep the area very cool. I only have seven boxes left to clean out; I saved them for when you arrived because they are going to be the most difficult to go through.

I just turned fifty years old, and I have been reflecting on my life's journey as people typically do on special landmark birthdays. I recognize that even though I feel young at heart, I am deteriorating physically. I've reached a point where I feel it is necessary to go through these boxes (some have filled up more recently than others) and deal with them. I have learned over the years that loss can be accepted or not accepted. From loss, we can retrieve and keep something valuable. Sometimes it is abstract like a life lesson, other times concrete like an item previously cherished by a loved one. When we lose a sentimental material object or give it away, it is like experiencing that loss all over again. I know that once each box is opened and gone through, the loss can be properly sorted, felt, and understood.

As odd as I know it sounds, my storage space is a sacred space to me. This unique location holds symbols of faith, hope, and love. I try to enter it reverently like a cemetery and leave it respectfully. It affords me almost a religious ritual of sorts in that I feel reconnected when I return to this space, and I have a sense of renewal as I go through the items of those that I have lost. Some of these items represent rites of passage in life such as confirmations, baptisms, weddings, and especially funerals. It is a sacred time for me. Every time I come here, I say a little storage prayer, and it always gives me peace. "Lord, give me peace as I desire to give generously and donate those things that you desire to move into someone else's hands. Help me to not be greedy. Help me to have the wisdom to keep the items that you have ordained as sacred for me to retain, and help me to trash the items that no longer serve their purpose. May I have no regrets in terms of giving, keeping, or disposing. I know I can't take it with me, and these things are temporal. Thank you. Amen."

I am sure that as you look around you may wonder why I would have ever bothered to have a storage unit in the first place. Why not just keep this stuff in the garage or a shed? The answer for me is simple really; the items in the boxes you see before you represent memories in limbo. On one hand, I don't want to remember them, and on the other hand, I don't want to forget them. For example, many of the items are photo albums and are, in essence, in picture purgatory. I don't want to be surrounded by them at home, but I am not ready to trash them quite yet. I don't want to remember them now, yet I don't want to forget them forever. As I look at the contents I feel a sense of how days and years melt into memorable moments represented by what I have retained. Sometimes I worry that I will get Alzheimer's and not be able to remember the life I have lived, so in essence, my mementos are my security blanket, visual memories of a life well lived.

I had multiple atypical, particularly difficult losses in the last ten years. Prior to these losses, I had the more typical losses of elderly grandparents, etc. With each loss, I have learned more about life, death, and myself. At times, my faith in God grew and was strong; at other times I struggled to find the positive aspect in my pain. At times, I was in survival mode, so I took the personal artifacts of those I lost, put them into boxes, and brought them here to store so I didn't have to deal with drama, but now that life has calmed down, I realize it is time to reflect on what I experienced. Some of the deaths were tidy. I knew that they were inevitable, as did the deceased. They made plans; I received items that were allocated to me. Others were very messy deaths, and the deceased left behind a hot mess for me to sort out during the chaotic aftermath.

So here I am the designated survivor of sorts. Sometimes it is lonely to be alone. Most days I wake up and joyfully proclaim, "This is the day the Lord has made; I will rejoice and be glad in it!" Yet, there are those anniversaries of death, birthdays, Mother's and Father's Day, Christmas, Thanksgiving, and Easter on which, even if spent in the presence of others, I feel painfully alone. It could be for a reason less obvious than the date on a calendar. It could be due to my hormones, or a memory brought on by a person who looks like my deceased loved one, or catching a whiff of a perfume that triggers a memory. In these moments, I sometimes mourn being the survivor.

Even though God is invisible, He has made Himself visible to me through the artifacts in these boxes that remind me of His unfailing love. Through the crisis, chaos, and confusion, these losses have all changed me in different ways, but my resiliency factor through them all has been my faith in God and, with Jesus, a confident expectation that I have hope for a brighter tomorrow.

No matter how the items came into my possession, one thing is clear. Physical things decay; photos fade, papers yellow, frames scratch, dried flowers deteriorate, and jewelry tarnishes. In essence, the things we use to remember the deceased pass away eventually, just as their owners did.

I know I can't move forward looking in the rearview mirror, but I believe there is a time and a place for glances, such as looking at that faded photo or using a visual reminder to recall a memory to honor the person I have lost and to reflect on the impact he/she had on me. It is not a stare, however; it is a glance, as I can't allow myself to not move forward. This is what my loved ones would want from me, so I must honor their request.

You know, it is somewhat ironic that we store our thoughts, feelings, and emotions in compartmentalized places like a storage box, but we also store these things in the compartmentalized places of our memories, hearts, and minds. We enter into these spaces sometimes planned, other times unplanned. Sometimes it brings us pain and sorrow, other times, joy and love. Sometimes we share our space; other times we close others out as I have a history of doing. However, today is different. Today I have decided to sweep my physical and mental space clean, and I have chosen to share my memories with you. Most of which have never been shared before. Thank you for helping me already unlock the door to my unit and to my heart. May you enjoy the journey with me, my friend.

1.

Jean's Box

The first box that I need to clean out today is plastic, pastel pink. It holds items to remind me of my best friend, Jean. I talked on the phone nightly with Jean for 25 years with rare exception. She was my best friend, counselor, confidante, role model, accountability partner, and sister in Christ.

In was January of 1985 when, a junior in high school, I entered my journalism class overwhelmed by the culture shock of moving from Minneapolis with my mom the week before. There were three editors of the school newspaper at the time. Two did not greet me at all. They were very pretty and went on to be the homecoming queens, one for Jean's senior year, and one for mine the next year. I was jealous of their looks, popularity, and wealth, none of which I possessed. I wished I were them. Later in life, as single moms, both died of breast cancer before the age of forty. I am glad I am I. The editor-in-chief, however, greeted me with a smile. She was a senior, and her name was Jean. Jean and I bonded right away, and although she graduated six months later, our friendship would span decades. On my first meeting with Jean, she created a map of the area for me, complete with all of the local fast food restaurants clearly labeled; I knew then that she was a woman after my own heart. I still cherish and use the map to this day.

Over the years, multiple moves have caused me to downsize, and now only three items remain in the box that holds memoirs of Jean. The first item a small, empty, silver box with card; the second a scrapbook I made of my special times with Jean; and the last, her eulogy.

The small silver heart-shaped box was given back and forth each year with the same birthday card for ten years. Usually our one-line entry would read, "This year is definitely going to be your year!" One year she wrote, "new job, new car, new church, you go girl! Here's hoping your 31st year brings a new Friday night date! Although your current 'Friday night date' will miss you dearly! I can't thank you enough for your friendship and prayers." We were each other's "Friday night date" for many years. One year I wrote, "Here's to remind you that there are many fish in the sea." Whatever was in the silver box was alluded to in the card, so I included a Christian fish symbol pin and goldfish crackers. She wrote, "I pray that age 34 brings good health, answers to prayer, and a wonderful 'August Man.'" She knew that August would get lonely for me; I was a teacher who had summers off. I always taught summer school, but I would still have August before the new school year began. She wrote to me, "Here's to your new condo and dogs, and no need for an August man. Celebrating the strength to move." To which I wrote the following year, "Here's to your new condo, kittens, and no need for any man, celebrating the strength to move on." When she turned forty I wrote, "You are over the hill! What a miracle!" This tradition occurred once in February and once in July, with something special in the silver box; small gifts such as angel pins, cross jewelry, bracelets, and earrings. I got this idea from my great-aunt, who passed the same card with her best friend for over fifty years; it is the one thing I inherited of my great aunt's after her passing, and I cherish it. Jean and I never got to the fifty-year mark—only ten years; we were robbed of our time together when cancer reared its ugly head. The silver box is now tarnished and empty. It fits into the palm of my hand. I hold it when I want to feel close to Jean, and on her birthday I consider what I would put in it to represent the past year and what I would write in the card to sum up the year in a witty fashion. The last entry reads from her to me, "One hour at a time in 2009. How does that sum up the first half of 2009? It is what it is." In the box was a black leather cord bracelet with a silver band that read, "It is what it is." To which I always verbally add her catch phrase after it, "but it becomes what we make it."

The second item in my Jean box is a photo album. Although over the course of knowing each other I married, divorced, and had a daughter, the majority of the time we were both single and made sure to keep each other company. Some years we were closer than others as we both were busy with college, our careers, family obligations, etc. Although we lived in close proximity to one another and spoke on the phone nightly, there were seasons when we rarely actually saw each other, especially while I was married and my daughter was a baby. When we did, we would always be sure to take pictures on our outings. We loved to take day trips. When we would go in public, we would sometimes get a disapproving stare. She had been on steroids due to cancer for quite some time, which really made her bulk up in spite of eating healthfully and exercising. She didn't have any hair, or at most, it was very short. We both liked to walk in comfortable shoes and clothes, and neither of us was really into makeup or into very feminine clothing. It probably didn't help much that I sent her a dozen roses at work once signed "Love, Bob." She said I didn't fool anyone. She had never received flowers before, so I thought it would brighten her day and calm the water cooler gossip about her love life; as it turns out, it did just the opposite, and rumors spread like wildfire about why I was sending her flowers. Once when we went to LEGOLAND together, we were laughing and carrying on and having a great time; a young female employee asked us what the nature of our relationship was. We didn't really grasp what she was insinuating at the time, but we just looked at each other, shrugged, and simultaneously said, "Best friends." People who knew us would be perplexed by the inquisition because one of our favorite lines was,

"If you were a guy, I'd marry you!" We both longed to be married. We used to joke that the pizza man had better watch out, or he would be pulled in to be the Friday night date. We tried to make light of our lack of male companionship. She bought me a "husband" (a large stuffed pillow that wraps around your back to support you in an upright position). I bought her a "grow-a-man" that you stick in water and he would emerge as your Prince Charming. I also got her Mr. Right, Mr. Perfect, and Mr. Wonderful dolls which, when you squeezed them, would say all the right things, like, "You are so thin; have some more ice cream!"

If Jean were a male, we couldn't marry in the church anyway, as Jean was a devout Catholic and I was not, but that didn't stop us from attending each other's churches and faith functions, as well as supporting each other spiritually and being each other's accountability partners. One day we visited the Lady of Angels church in Los Angeles. The sanctuary was packed. We were ushered onto the stage area next to where the priest stands for mass. I was clueless as to all the protocol of the event, and I felt like I was sitting in the spotlight.

The priest came down the center aisle with burning incense that had a strong aroma. It was actually overwhelming, and those around the priest looked concerned that something may have gone wrong. Jean broke out into a terrible hacking cough, being overwhelmed by the fumes, as the priest approached his spot in front of us. Gagging, she made a run for the door. I was unable to go after her due to being blocked on stage by the priest. In a hushed whisper I pleaded, "Don't leave me; I don't know what to do!" She responded through sputters, "Just follow the nuns!" That is exactly what I did. They were in the front row on the side. When they stood, I stood. When they sat, I sat. When they kneeled, I kneeled. They were amazing role models.

Not long after, we went to a concert in the park. Behind us on a blanket sat a group of young nuns who were singing, dancing, and carrying on in a loud manner, very unlike the quiet behavior you would expect from nuns. Therefore, I started singing and dancing, and Jean said, "What are you doing?" I replied, "I am just following the nuns."

This photo album is chock full of special memories. I am so glad that I lived in an era of developing printed pictures and putting them in scrapbooks and albums. Today a person takes a picture and leaves it on a digital cloud, never to be revisited. I am equally glad that we lived in a time prior to the popularity of cell phones. We didn't text one another because it was before the time when that came into vogue. We actually talked on the phone, holding a tangible, weighted item, lying on the bed like we were teenagers and having deep, meaningful conversations instead of one-word interactions between the "Can you hear me nows?" We had one of those special, unique relationships where it didn't matter how long it had been since you actually saw the other person; when you got together, it was as if no time had passed at all, and you were bonded.

Jean and I loved to go out to eat, and since we didn't have anyone to go out to dine with, that frequently meant that we would share a meal. Here is one of my favorite pictures of Jean, the last time we went out to eat together. She is holding up her favorite chocolate pizookie at B.J.s. We followed the adage, "Life is uncertain, eat dessert first." We attributed much of her beating cancer for so long to Girl Scout Thin Mint cookies and Dreyer's matching ice cream of the same name. For one birthday, we went to the Melting Pot and had to use the spoon to "fish out" our fondue items that fell in the pot more than eat off the skewer.

Here is another favorite picture of the last one of my birthdays we celebrated together. We went to a very fancy restaurant, which was unusual for us. They only had expensive gourmet seafood items on the menu. I asked if they had any chicken, to which the waiter replied, "If you want chicken, we will send for some aircraft chicken." We joked about what airliner was sending in the chicken, and how it must be coming from quite a distance because it was taking so long. We took our traditional photo where we held up the menu of wherever we were. We held it in front of our necks and asked, "How many chins do I have?" After about an hour, the waiter returned out of breath with a beautifully plated gourmet chicken entree, and I still wonder to this day where he flew it in from.

Not only did we love our favorite pastime, eating; we also shared the love of musicals, Jesus, contemporary Christian music, *Little House on the Prairie*, animals, talking on the phone, giving to others, and traveling.

After her diagnosis, we started working on completing Jean's bucket list of items that she wanted to accomplish before her death. Toward the top of the list was to see the Grand Canyon. We took a train overnight. I woke up in the middle of the night and found her in the fetal position on the train floor. The jarring ride really exacerbated her cancer pain, but she was determined to make the journey.

We did a one-day car rental in a small town. The car had to be back by nine p.m. It was a mom and pop business, with about three cars to rent. We were probably driving a family member's car. They made a big deal of our getting the car back in time. Jean was the driver. Thanks to my lack of navigational skills, we got lost quite a few times, and it was rapidly approaching the nine o'clock hour. Jean was typically a slow driver, never one to break the law, and always punctual. We were in a remote area. To take our minds off the fact that we were lost and late, she blared her favorite musical, *The Sound of Music*, and we sang "Our Favorite Things" at the top of our lungs as she raced at a very high speed down the road. We laughed so hard we cried.

The next day we did a pink Jeep tour. I informed them of Jean's situation and requested a modified tour that was gentle and would just drive us around to the sites for photo ops. The young driver had a different idea of what a smooth ride meant, and he sped off into the sunset with us bouncing around in the back. I looked over and saw tears rolling down Jean's face from under her sunglasses. I asked the driver to pull over for a rest. Jean never said a word about her pain, not wanting to ruin the moment. She even finished the private tour. She frequently suffered in silence for the benefit of others.

Here is a picture of us on the last trip we took together in San Diego.

We rode on a pedicab. The back of the driver's shirt read, "Stop staring at my butt." How did he know Jean said he was a "cutie patootie"? After indulging at Ghirardelli Square in the Gaslamp district, we stayed the night. We shared a hotel room, with two queen beds. I didn't sleep a wink, as Jean groaned in pain loudly all night long. She could not find rest from pain, even in her sleep. I knew then that the end was near.

I have hundreds of pictures, always thinking, for 12 years, that each outing would be our last. We enjoyed day tripping together to Mission San Juan Capistrano, where we always stopped by the St. Peregrine room, lit a candle, and said a prayer for Jean and her friends from chemo who had preceded her in death. There were so many that I often thought that it was not about *if* you get cancer, but *when you get cancer*. I was worried that I was going to turn into a hypochondriac. Every little pain I had, in my mind, must be terminal cancer. Jean made me promise that I would get a yearly mammogram, knowing that I don't really go to doctors. I have reluctantly kept my promise every year.

We just loved spending time together! We loved to frequent Downtown Disney. I had a memorial brick placed at Disneyland to commemorate our friendship and love of all things Disney.

This is a picture of us at the Getty museum. That was a memorable experience. They were having a stained-glass window exhibit, and neither of us had ever been there before, so we decided to help get her mind off things and have a day trip. Jean was hurting, not only from cancer, but also from a broken heart. There was one guy named Sean. They were both my friends from high school, Catholic, went to the same church, and were neighbors, but they had never met, so I took it upon myself to introduce them later in life. They bonded right away. She informed me that I would need to foot the bill for therapy when her relationship was over with him, because he was so perfect he would surely leave her. I know Jean loved him. It was more of an unrequited love where they were the best of friends, and like siblings, but cancer stole Jean's dream of marriage and children, so it never developed into what it might have been. To Sean's credit, he was a terrific distraction in the midst of the realities of cancer, and he stopped by her house every night on his way home from work to give her the required nightly shot and check on her. That I could have never done, nor would she have ever asked, so I am glad for his presence in her life. He was the only man Jean ever loved in that way.

Here is my favorite picture of Jean with Sean standing on my front lawn on Easter, dressed in their Sunday best. Jean looked so beautiful, and happy. Jean never really dated anyone else. She was conservative in dress and lifestyle, and although all loved her, she was never loved by one. She would joke with tongue in cheek about who would want a bald woman, stuffed with steroids, who has a slightly lighter breast on the left side? I know it was the guys' loss more than it was hers.

A few months later, it seemed clear that cancer would rob her of a serious relationship with Sean, as he seemed frightened to get involved in that way, for which I can't say I blame him. Jean found out that Sean was dating someone, and it had become serious. We went to the Getty to distract her from the reality that cancer had stolen something other than her health, her looks, her chance at having children, and life, something more important to her—true love. As we were exiting, a polite, well-dressed man opened the door for us to proceed through. It was Sean! Behind him was the woman he was dating. I wanted to "just smile and wave," as Jean used to say, but in a moment that was so characteristically Jean she introduced herself with such grace. She hugged the girl, spent the entire time conversing and encouraging her, as Sean was so nervous and caught off guard that he kept talking to me and ignoring Jean. He was humiliated because he knew Jean had intense feelings for him. After what seemed like an eternity of awkwardness, we parted ways and walked to the car. In true Jean fashion, she spoke very highly of Sean's date, but I knew she was choking back tears. She couldn't have even one day of reprieve from her physical or emotional pain, but she did not complain. She had purchased a CD of monks chanting and coughing (probably from excessive incense) in a live recording in a remote village in Italy. We turned it on and listened to it in silence all the way home.

Although sometimes painful to view, one of my favorite pictures is of Sean, Jean, and me from the park in their neighborhood. Flying a kite was on Jean's bucket list, so we decided to make it happen. We swung on the swings, and it was Sean's and my job to get the kite off the ground. Jean was in a lot of pain at this time and feeling very ill from the chemo, and we were determined to get that kite to fly. Sean and I gave up after about an hour of looking like the Charlie Browns of the kite flying community. Jean stood up and said, "We are going to get this kite to fly." Within a few short minutes, Jean got it to soar! She exclaimed with one of her Jeanisms, "Go big, or go home!" Jean was one of those people who always knew what to do.

Cancer did not only rob Jean of a husband and children, it robbed her of some family and friends. It is especially difficult for some family members due to the constant visual reminder that your family member is suffering, and you share genetic bonds that may negatively affect you as well. No one wanted Jean's genes. People are uncomfortable talking about cancer because it is associated with pain, disease, and death. There is so much stigma attached to those topics in our society. Jean suffered for 12 years. People were afraid to ask her how she was; although she always answered positively, the water cooler gossip knew better. She wanted to share pictures of traveling with her husband, and family portraits with her children. She wasn't even eligible to adopt due to her condition. She was not allowed to have an online dating profile without lying about her illness, which she never would do. She was at that stage of life, and everyone wanted a family for her, but all she had was a collection of wigs and a giant file of medical papers to pass around.

Sometimes people would say the wrong thing, instead of saying no-thing. She made people feel comfortable with the uncomfortable. Jean was also one of those rare people who knew exactly what to say, at exactly the right moment, and even the prickliest of people loved and respected her ability to affirm all in her presence. She had many sayings that we called "Jeanisms" that became a part of our everyday vernacular. One of my favorites was, "Stick a fork in me—I'm done."

Nevertheless, she wasn't done yet. Jean's biggest bucket list item was to travel to Italy and see the Pope. A friend of hers was going, and invited her. The doctor reluctantly agreed but said they had to keep it quick, so off they went. I was admittedly jealous that I couldn't go with them. I asked for a souvenir "Pope on a Rope." I had seen on TV that it was a popular souvenir item. It was a carving of the bust of the pope in soap connected to a rope for the shower. Jean said that she thought it was probably sacrilege, and jokingly added that she didn't want to be struck down by lightening in the papal presence. Nonetheless, being a connoisseur of all things tchotchkes, I wanted it. She called me from Rome to check in and let me know that she had arrived safely although not feeling well, and the weather and walking didn't help. She was trying to remain positive, as always. It was the day she was to see the Pope; he was making an appearance, and the whole trip had been scheduled around this event. I later found out that Jean was not able to attend. She stubbed her big toe on the side of the bed, and it ripped off her entire toenail and did significant damage to her toe! She bled a lot due to her medications, and even though she was a trooper she was unable to hobble through the crowds to see His Eminence. So close, and yet so far . . . Jean would have been so honored to be in the Pope's presence. However, I believe that if *he* had known *she* was in the audience, he would have been honored to be graced by hers.

I didn't get a Pope on a Rope after all, but I did get a calendar of "Hot Priests." I guess on the overall scale of blasphemy, it was on a much lower ranking. Loved it! The gift kept on giving all year long. Pope on a Rope couldn't hold a candle to it.

Another item on Jean's bucket list was to walk across the Golden Gate Bridge. This seemed like a doable dream, so she headed off with her family. She called me to relay the events of the day. I eagerly anticipated hearing about the view and the experience in general. Jean was very melancholy and not at all herself. I had to pull the information out of her. I sensed something was terribly wrong. I figured it was a health-related episode, but I was shocked to hear of her experience.

Jean did indeed walk on the Golden Gate Bridge. She stopped to take a picture, and a young man in his twenties passed her slowly. She said hi, and he nodded, and then proceeded to jump off the bridge in an instant right next to her. He committed suicide right in front of her, and Jean witnessed it all. She had to recount the event numerous times to the authorities. How ironic that a person who fought daily for 24 hours due to physical illness witnessed the death of a young person whose life was cut short due to mental illness. Physical and mental pain both erode the will to continue. Jean was the last person he interacted with. If they would have had a moment to talk, I am sure it would have made a difference; Jean had that way about her. What struck me was that she was not at all judgmental of the young man committing suicide, but she was reflecting on her own mortality. Tragic for him, traumatic for her. From the Golden Gate to the Pearly Gate in an instant.

The realities of Jean's declining health status progressed over 12 years. She was diagnosed with breast cancer the day before her 31st birthday and died at age 43. The cancer journey was long and arduous. It ebbed and flowed over the years with radiation, surgeries, and experimental drugs, spreading from her breast to her spine and then to major organs. Her diet became so restrictive due to medications and health concerns. She would get out of breath so easily, and become weak. The pain was robbing her of her quality of life more and more. We couldn't even go out to eat anymore, as everything made her sick to her stomach. We longed for the days in the beginning of the journey of being able to go wig shopping to cover her head, bald from chemo. Some of the sales women were so rude and inconsiderate; it made it hard for me to be respectful and kind to them, but at least we were out and about, if for the most difficult of tasks. We rode the escalator up and down, as Jean was uncharacteristically indecisive about what wig she wanted. At first, I thought she was being frugal, as wigs are expensive, but later I realized that the lack of desire to make a purchase was due to the diagnosis becoming a reality of a completely new world that she did not want to travel through.

After Jean passed, I purchased her car, the "Jean mobile," from the family. It was special to me, as we shared many great times in that Toyota. Just prior to her death, she went into the parking lot as her brother drove her car to see it turn over to 100,000 miles. A milestone marking the miles of a life well lived. One day, I opened a small compartment in the car that I had overlooked previously, and there were some change, hairpins, and wig barrettes that she had purchased when I was with her during that first wig shopping excursion right after she was diagnosed. I cried; our beautiful journey, marked by many miles, was over.

I vividly remember the beginning of the journey when I received the call. Jean and I played a game every night for 12 years called "You win!" We would each share the events of the day. Whoever had the worst day with the most drama was the winner. Due to my issues and ongoing personal crisis, I would win easily most days. To which Jean would exclaim, "Winnah, winnah, lobstah dinnah!" "High five from Jean!" This night, Jean's voice sounded panicked. "I found a lump in my breast while showering." I responded, "Don't panic, it is probably a cyst. You don't have a family history, and you are otherwise healthy. You are so young; you just turned 31. You don't even need mammograms yet; just make a doctor's appointment. You will be fine." When I hung up. however, I thought to myself, *Sorry Jean, you win.*

After the needed tests, the doctor inquired, "Do you have any children?" Although this had been her lifelong dream, Jean responded in the negative.

"Thank God you don't have kids. You have six weeks to live." He walked out the door.

What?! I quickly searched for a second opinion, and I found one. A premier oncologist whose mother and sister died of breast cancer. We cornered him at his book signing the next day, and he agreed to see Jean. Although his deadpan bedside manner barely exceeded the previous doctor's, he did have some strategies up his sleeve that he thought might extend her life, and indeed did.

The chemo room had an odor of death and chemicals. It was a

morose place of irony, the inhabitants in the act of living while dying, and dying while living. This would be her sentence every week for 12 years. Her oncologist was also a noted researcher. She was the test rat for every experimental drug available at that time. During Jean's tenure, she would have two amazing primary nurses; over time both were diagnosed with cancer in their thirties. One survived, while the other did not. The one who did not had a sister who died of the same shortly after her death. I will never forget the look on their parents' faces at the funeral. Losing both of their daughters to the same disease before they even hit forty years of age.

As a person who hates hospitals, needles, and all things medical, I was constantly seeking distraction in that den of torture called the chemo lounge. I struck up a conversation with the regular patient next to Jean who was a young mother with breast cancer. Her name was Robyn. She believed that she had developed cancer from stress. She had taken her family to a beach bonfire party. Her son was young, preschool aged, and playing amongst the crowd when he fell into the fire pit. She felt a lot of guilt regarding his barely surviving and experiencing third-degree burns all over his body. Once she fought for his life, and she found herself now fighting for her own life. Robyn and Jean had a lot in common, including their faith, and we came to look forward to chatting during treatments.

One day during treatment, Jean had an excruciatingly painful experience while hooked up to her "chemo cocktail." She was experiencing a serious and painful allergic reaction. She handled it with such grace, not wanting to scare anyone. Robyn was sitting in the treatment chair next to her; I was standing and praying. Suddenly Robyn yelled at the top of her lungs, "FUCK CANCER!" One by one, the women in the room started screaming in kind. The room was filled with a cacophony of moans, groans, screams, and yells. Jean and I never used profanity, but I felt their pain. Two weeks later, Robyn died. Two months later, her nine-year-old son died of a broken heart. He missed his mom so much; he gave up the will to fight to fully recover from all of his burn scars and painful treatments and surgeries. All I could think was, "Fuck cancer."

There were survivors. A bell hung over the chemo room exit door. When you were free, free of cancer, free of chemo, free from pain, never to return, you got to ring the freedom bell, and everyone cheered. Every week for 12 years, Jean passed under the bell and looked up longingly. Every time we passed through I said, "Next week is going to be your week," to which she would respond, "From your mouth to God's ear."

Over 12 years, repeated chemo, radiation, surgeries, scans, and doctors' appointments take a toll on a person. Jean never faltered, always full of grace and kindness for all. She didn't even "play the cancer card," so she gave me permission to play it on her behalf. While we were on the phone, the other line would buzz in. It would be a salesperson. I would shut them down by saying, "I am on the other line with my best friend who has terminal cancer. I have to go, and I don't want to keep her waiting." It worked every time.

I had read a book about what to do if your friend has cancer, and one of the recommendations was to ask her if she wanted to talk about it or if she wanted a distraction. I had plenty of drama to distract her with. This suggestion proved to be very helpful to us both over the years. Other than listening and providing a distraction, my primary contribution was to pray for her. I also attended her major doctor visits.

On October 1, 2009, I went to the doctor with her to get her latest scan results. The cancer had spread to her bones and liver previously. Although now, over the years, the doctor was like family, his serious demeanor was a constant. He said that the latest round of chemotherapy was ineffective. The silence was palpable. Out of nervous energy I said, "Well, at least we now know what doesn't work."

He turned to Jean and said, "We all need more friends like her." He went on to say, "The problem is that nothing works, and we are out of options. Your liver has stopped functioning."

To which Jean responded, "Give me a year? (Silence). Six months?

(Silence). Three months? (Silence). You are thinking, Jean, I gave you 12 years—what more do you want?"

He replied, "I am sorry. Goodbye, Jean," and walked out of the room just like that. Hospice started the next day.

As much as Jean had planned to die for 12 years, she wasn't prepared to be rendered a death sentence.

Oct. 7th, 7:00 p.m.: the answering machine beeped . . . I heard Jean crying and dry heaving into the phone; although she didn't really speak, I knew it was her.

Oct. 7th, 8:00 p.m.: beep . . . "Sorry to have left you such a pathetic message. Please erase it so you don't remember me that way."

I already had erased it. I was already feeling the loss, and she was still alive.

Oct. 10th, 8:00 p.m.: Jean and I spoke on the phone. She had sent away the hospice workers because they were so intense. She had a nurse who continued to have to do painful procedures to prepare for her demise. The nurse expressed concern because of her continual dry heaving that was not an expected side effect of the medication. The nurse asked her what specifically was upsetting her because they needed the dry heaving to stop. She said it was because she was worried about saying goodbye to me. She knew I was facing many serious challenges in life, and she knew that I was alone in the journey. Here again, Jean was thinking of me, and not herself. The nurse advised her to meet with me and get it over with, so she could be at peace and keep medication down. Little did Jean know that I had been dry heaving continuously as well, due to the same reason. I even had severe sympathetic breast pain in the location where her cancer began. This on top of continual nightmares. I was a hot mess.

Oct. 11th: I visited Jean for an hour and a half for the last time. We looked at photo albums together. I tried to console her by reminding her that her parents would be waiting for her in heaven, and she said that really helped her mindset. She had been the primary caregiver to both of her elderly parents during their long-term illnesses. She asked me to write and deliver her eulogy. She expressed concern about me not having any support system in my life and the personal crisis I was experiencing on an ongoing basis. She told me that as soon as she got to heaven, the first thing she was going to do was start lining up men for me on earth. Curious at the prospect, I asked, "How will I know they are from you?" To which she responded with a smile, "He will be Catholic." With that, our time was up. I walked to the door, gave her a hug, smiled and said, "I will see you again." I walked through the door, and turned around and shouted, "Hey Jean, we didn't even vomit." To which I heard a small chuckle in the distance. I cried the whole way home while driving and listening to praise music.

Oct. 27th. Time passed, I had the flu, and her nurse wouldn't let me visit. I secretly although ashamedly was relieved, as I just didn't have the strength physically or emotionally to see her. Jean didn't want me to visit, because she said on the phone that she now had peace, and she could "settle in to what lies before her." There were other friends who would not leave her bedside, some of whom she had not even been that close to. She privately confided in me that they were driving her crazy, but in true Jean fashion she felt they needed to do it for their own mental health and grief process. So she didn't say anything, although tempted to say one of her favorite Jeanisms, "Here's your hat; what's your hurry?"

We spoke briefly on the phone due to her pain. The last thing she said to me is, "Are you okay? How is everything?" She was knocking on death's door and asking how I was. She was a saint in my eyes. She had to go without hearing a response, as she was in too much pain. I found myself feeling guilty over my selfishness in praying that she would die at a convenient time for me. I had a new job, and getting off work to deliver the eulogy and attend services was not going to be easy. I started walking and journaling as stress relievers, to help me prepare for the new chapter I was about to start.

I tried retail therapy to purchase a black dress for the funeral but found myself in tears when an acquaintance from the past ran into me at Kohl's and asked how I was. Although I am typically not an emotional person, or one who cries at all, all the pain and sadness of my life overwhelmed me at that question, and I sobbed so hard I couldn't respond. I was so embarrassed I left empty-handed. Poor woman. I am sure she will never again ask someone how he or she is doing.

Oct. 31st: Jean died. I got the call from her sister. She sat in silence on the phone. I finally asked, "Is Jean with Jesus?" To which she cried as I had done in Kohl's. I got it.

Afterward all I wanted to do was sleep, stuff my face, and sulk. Jean would never have had that; she would have expected more of me, and so I will starve, stroll, and smile.

The third and final item is the eulogy I wrote for her funeral, titled "What Would Jean Do?"

Thank you for joining us as we honor Jean's life, her uniqueness, her own special gifts that she shared with the rest of the world. We are celebrating Jean's life, her connections with family and friends and those who loved her. I have the honor of reading words prepared by Jean for this event. As you know, Jean was a planner, so it is no surprise that she planned for this occasion as well:

"Goodbye: Wow. What can I say? If you are reading this, my battle with cancer is over. Please know that I am in a better place, and my body is whole. I can't thank you enough for all you did for me. I know, after my taking care of Mom and Dad, that you were burdened at least emotionally by my illness and life. I also know that God could have called me home much earlier than He did. I am thankful that I was born and that I was able to enjoy so much of my life. I am so thankful for my family, friends, coworkers, and caregivers. I pray that I touched each of you in some memorable way."

Jean was born on February 2, 1967, in Lakewood, California. Her strong Catholic family consisted of two loving parents. She was the youngest sibling of two girls and two boys. Jean attended Lakewood High School, where she won the Spanish award and was editor of the newspaper. She went on to graduate from California State University, Long Beach, with a Bachelor's in Business. She was a member of St. Cornelius church and later attended St. Joseph's parish.

Jean was a 12-year cancer survivor, having been diagnosed with breast cancer one week before her 31st birthday. She had no family history of the disease. Later the disease developed into bone and liver cancer. She went home to Jesus at 7:30 a.m. on Saturday, October 31, 2009. The ending is rather poetic, as October is National Breast Cancer Awareness month. Jean was born on Groundhog's Day and died on Halloween, the day before All Saints' Day, two days before Day of the Dead. Her mother was born on Valentine's Day and died on Christmas. Her family has an affinity for holidays! Leave it to Jean to even die perfectly. I am sure no one here is one bit surprised, as she always did everything right.

Jean made jokes (a true sign of her resilience) when there were times of crisis. I know she would want her memoir to be light, so please indulge me as I make a feeble attempt to emulate her witty character.

For those of you who don't know, her favorite color was blue; her favorite shape, a heart; favorite animal, a cat (she had two that she regarded as her fur babies: Hope and Faith, who incidentally cuddled up with her postmortem in her bed while awaiting the coroner. Although young, they died not long after of broken hearts). Her favorite flower, a tulip; favorite collection, angels; favorite dessert, a chocolate pizookie at B.J.'s; favorite TV series, *Little House on the Prairie*; favorite musical, *The Sound of Music* (a little known fact: Jean had a beautiful voice.) Although she had many favorite "Jeanisms," her favorite saying was, "It is what it is . . . ," and I would close with, "but it becomes what we make it." Those are her stats, but if you are here it is because you know Jean on a different level. You probably know Jean as a family member, friend, coworker, neighbor, patient, community, or church member.

As a patient, Jean kept her doctor's office on their toes. Her intellect and wit made her a self-advocate with a loving demeanor. Who would be a patient patient while enduring excruciating pain? JEAN WOULD.

A special thanks to her doctors and staff, as well as the hospice workers who assisted Jean.

As a community and church member, Jean was an outstanding citizen giving freely of her time, talent, and treasure. She attended church weekly, and she was not a "Sunday Christian"; she was a 24/7 Christian. She donated her treasure privately and generously to many nonprofits, including her favorite, Breast Cancer Angels.

She donated her talent in writing and sponsoring Yan-Yan, a young Chinese girl, through World Vision. Incidentally, when Jean found out that the end was near, she paid through Yan-Yan's 18th birthday in advance to make sure she would be provided for. Who would think of others first while dying? JEAN WOULD.

She donated her time (the most valuable resource, and who can say that more than Jean?) to CASA (Court Appointed Student Advocate). She mentored two little girls by spending her every healthy weekend with them taking them on field trips throughout the community.

This is just a partial list of her charitable deeds; it would take us all day to enumerate all of her benevolence, but you get the picture. Who would donate their time when it is knowingly limited? JEAN WOULD.

Who would donate money in this economy, and when there are medical bills to pay? Say it if you know it. JEAN WOULD.

Who would donate talent and not be compensated for it? JEAN WOULD.

Jean was an outstanding neighbor. She visited previous neighbors and gave them her time when she was physically able. Who would take the time nowadays to do that? JEAN WOULD.

She loved being a member of a community and reaching her goal of owning a condominium.

Thank you to her neighbors and community members who watched out for her. A special thank you to her fellow church members for praying for her.

Jean was also a superior coworker. She worked at the same aerospace company for 18 years. She felt like her peers were another family. She said through a rare instance of tears, "I just want to go back to work." I thought, *Clearly, she must be seriously ill, because who would say they WANT to go to work?* JEAN WOULD.

Thank you to her coworkers and especially supervisors who looked at the person above the payroll.

There are those like myself who knew Jean as a friend. When the seventy's singing siblings Donny and Marie Osmond's mother recently died, the eldest of numerous siblings stood up at the funeral and said, "I was my mom's favorite child." The audience stirred. He repeated, "No, it's true. I was my mom's favorite child. I know you feel like you could say that is true of yourself, and I know this, because she made every child feel like her favorite." When I heard this, I thought, *That is Jean. I am Jean's best friend.* I bet many of you in this audience take offense to that remark, but what is true of Mrs. Osmond is true of Jean; she made each one of us feel like her best friend. Like we were the only one who mattered. Who could do that? JEAN COULD.

I could NEVER list all of the friends Jean had. If Jean attended, organized, or was in your wedding or baby shower, please raise your hand. True, she was always a bridesmaid and never a bride, always a godmother, never a mom, but no one could fill her shoes. Who could stand to go to all those wedding and bridal showers and play all of those party games with a smile? JEAN COULD.

To her friends, I am sure you share my sentiment when I say that I was never the friend to Jean that she was to me. Wow! What a priceless gift we were given! Thank you for being friends not just for the road, but also for the journey. Ladies, I would like to keep her memory alive by keeping in touch and meeting on occasion to share our favorite Jeanisms. Please be sure to sign the gal pal contact sheet if you would be interested in joining me.

Last, but certainly not least, Jean's role as a family member. Jean's family was her pride and joy. She endured the hardship of the passing of both of her parents. She spoke fondly and frequently of them.

I am sure that you would agree that Jean was a success. Ralph Waldo Emerson, American philosopher, essayist, and poet, defined success as "to laugh often and much, to win the respect of intelligent people, and affection of children; to earn the appreciation of honest critics, and endure the betrayal of false friends; to appreciate beauty, to find the best in others; to leave the world a bit better, whether by a healthy child, a garden patch, or a redeemed social condition, to know even one life has breathed easier because you have lived. This is to have succeeded."

Kay Henley wrote a poem titled "I Was Born for a Purpose." In coming to a close, I would like to share it with you, inserting Jean's name for "I."

Jean was born for a purpose
To do something right
To provide inspiration
To show Christ's life
Jean was born for a reason
To make changes in this world
To proclaim our Lord and Savior,
To tell people God's word
Jean was born in this time
Determined by God above.
He wanted her spirit here and now
To tell of Christ's love.
Jean was born for a purpose
Born for this time

God gave her life
He had a purpose in mind!

Although Jean was never a wife or mother, much to her cha-grin, she was a person born for a purpose. It was her daily cross to bear her cancer with faith, hope, strength, courage, and love, knowing that Christian and non-believer alike were watching. She would express concern about not being a good witness to God's grace. To me, she was the model Christian. If you are not a Chris-tian, maybe you won't spend time thinking about the old adage "What would Jesus do?" However, perhaps we can bring honor to her name thinking, "What would Jean do?" Today, I briefly shared what Jean would do. She loved others unconditionally. She loved others in spite of who they were, not because of who they were.

My challenge to us all is to keep Jean's memory alive. Every time we do a race for the cure, or donate money to the cause, every time we are that special friend, and act selflessly. Every time we embrace work, and those who are toiling there with us. Every time we visit a neighbor in need. Every time we give a card, send an email, or call a family member. Every time we show compassion to an animal, or a child—THAT IS WHAT JEAN WOULD DO. I trust that God greeted her at the pearly gates and said, "Well done, my good and faithful servant—well done."

First Corinthians 13:13 says, "And now these three remain: faith, hope and love. But the greatest of these is love." Now may we all go forth in faith, hope, and love in remembrance and honor to the greatest patient, neighbor, community and church member, coworker, friend, and family member we have ever had the honor of knowing. Thank you for this privilege. May Peace be with you.

My daughter closed the service singing, as Jean had requested. Cancer ravages the body in such a way that it makes the viewing unpleasant, but she did have on the angel necklace I gave her with the words "hope" and "faith" on it. The eulogy went well. The priest said it was the best he had ever heard. I couldn't help but giggle to myself when I saw that the priest wore torn-up sneakers. I wanted to call Jean at 8:00 p.m., as I had for the last 25 years, and tell her all about it, to which she would respond, "That's classic!"

Instead, I called her voicemail and listened to her outgoing message repeatedly. I even left her a message once. I just had to call her back and let her know that I got her message. You see, the day after she died, I heard the phone ring, and the voicemail picked up, as I didn't want to speak to anyone. Jean and I always let voicemail answer the phone so we could decide if we wanted to talk to the person on the other end of the line. To alert one another that it was us, we would say, "It's me—Are you there?" Over and over in a repetitive, jovial style, trying to get the person to pick up faster. Now through the message machine I heard, "It's me—Are you there?" At that moment, a bell went off in my head, and I knew that Jean was free. My daughter and I were talking about missing Jean, so I know it wasn't my imagination because she heard it as well.

Oct. 31, 2019: Today is the ten-year anniversary of Jean's death. As I read this memoir to Jean at her gravesite and pour a coke over her grave (she does not need to suffer through Diet Coke anymore), I am still striving to be the friend and person to others that she was to me. Jean taught me so much about how to live; I am eternally grateful.

Not surprisingly, Jean made good on her promise one year after she died. It was perfect timing in my life. It took me a year to grieve the loss of Jean, and I was now ready to move forward. I met a wonderful man. We both worked in the same school district. He was a teacher, and we had similar educational backgrounds. He never tires of my "Jean memories" and didn't even falter when I told him that he was an answer to prayer (no pressure!); he has even met her family and friends.

He takes pink tulips to her gravesite with me at least twice a year. I just wanted to call Jean and let her know that I had met my prince charming after 16 years of being single. Instead, we announced our engagement at her gravesite, which is very close to our house, and I showed her my ring. "Our prayers were answered! Mr. Right had arrived!" Every time we drive by, I say aloud, "Hi Jean! Miss you! Wish you were here! I am having a great time!" Now I am happily married to an amazing man chosen by Jean and sent by God. How do I know Jean chose him? Well, that is easy: he is Catholic.

I could never list all of her life lessons that she bestowed upon me, but here are a few:

1. Generosity and Benevolence—Put others first. Invest your time, talent, and treasure into others.
2. Modesty and Humility—Give in secret, and don't be afraid to step out of the spotlight, and work from the shadows.
3. Hope and Faith—Project hope and faith into every situation.
4. Humor and Intellect—Use your wit in crisis to encourage others.
5. Most importantly—Follow the nuns.

2.
Paul's Box

The second box I need to clean out today is a black, plastic file bin. It holds three items to remind me of my favorite student, Paul. In it, I have pictures, newspaper articles, and funeral/memorial bulletins for ten middle and high school students I was blessed to know in my capacity as a professional school counselor.

I started my career straight out of college at age 21. Over the course of 25 years in K–12 education, I was a fourth- and fifth-grade teacher, a special education Mild/Moderate Special Education teacher, and a professional school counselor spanning all grade levels over my tenure. I worked in an affluent private Christian school, and amongst migrant workers in the central coast of California, meeting with parents as they picked strawberries in the fields. Over the years, the students and their families taught me more than I could ever teach them.

Although I did switch schools frequently, as I easily get bored, and I was always looking for a new opportunity to learn and grow, I did stay at one middle school for ten years as my daughter attended the elementary school next door and then my school for junior high. This afforded me as a single mom to have the best vantage point for my professional and personal worlds. I loved my school and students, and I was soon promoted from special education teacher to department head to professional school counselor to lead counselor for all of the district's K–8 schools. Under the tutelage of an outstanding school principal, paired with an amazing administration team and school psychologist, I experienced exponential professional development that led me to win counseling awards, including the coveted American School Counselor Association RAMP (Recognized ASCA Model Program) Award, signifying our exemplary school counseling program that I led. From that, my principal nominated me for the ASCA School Counselor of the Year, where I came in first semi-finalist for the nation.

Professional school counselors work with students individually, in small groups, in classroom settings as well as in crisis counseling. We support students in the three domains of academic, college/career, and personal/social/emotional success. Our roles include leader, systems change agent, advocate, and consultant/collaborator/coordinator.

Although the American School Counselor Association (ASCA) recommends a 250 student-to-counselor ratio, my first year I was the only one for 1,500 diverse students in a large urban school district from which I had also graduated high school. I spent my days being reactive instead of proactive, dealing with child abuse cases and self-harm, as well as suicidal and homicidal ideation. I was working long hours and found myself suffering from compassion fatigue at the end of each workday, only to meet with more drama in my personal life once I got home. I felt depleted, but I knew in my heart that God had given me this privilege and responsibility to my students and their families as a ministry, and I needed Him every step of the way to get through the next decade.

One day I doubted my work was making a difference, and I was feeling frustrated and exhausted. A student of mine had lied to me about having cancer. I figured it out after I had done everything I could to get her and her family the assistance they needed, including using personal finances and rallying the financial support of other benevolent people. This same week, I had a student who did have cancer, and no one would believe her. It was a rare form of cancer, and she was even taken to many specialists and a psychologist. Her family turned away from her; they believed she was seeking attention. Turns out her instincts were correct, and she was now in a medical crisis because the cancer had spread due to its not having been detected earlier. I was hurt, angry, and emotionally spent, so I took my daughter to Chuck E. Cheese so she could have fun while I just drowned myself in cheese. The mouse himself came out, stood on a table, and yelled, "When I say Chuck E., you say Cheese!" "Chuck E." "Cheese!" "Chuck E." "Cheese!" everyone gleefully responded. This looked to me like my dream job. Everyone loved Chuck E. Cheese. He wasn't responsible for saving lives, only bringing joy into others' lives. I got an application and filled it out. Turned out I was too old and overqualified, and they had no interest in hiring me. This was probably for the best; I would probably have fallen off the table, and my daughter and I would have had to live on pizza, as that would have been all we could afford if I had tried to support us both on minimum wage.

I relented after a good tearful prayer and went back to work the next day. I had to get a strategy not only to survive but also to thrive. I had to implement some self-care into my daily routine. I started journaling my experiences to help me mentally compartmentalize work and home. I started walking daily. I started a "feel good" file in my cabinet, where I placed every picture and thank you card that students and their families made for me, so I could reflect on them when I was having a particularly challenging day. I started a journal to record answers to prayer to build my faith, and have a visual representation of what God was doing in my life on a daily basis.

I had to set professional and personal boundaries, which was difficult for me, as I was a people pleaser who didn't know how to say no. I had to create an emotional distance to a certain extent between my students and me. As the saying goes, "In the event of an emergency, place the breathing mask over your own face first, before attempting to save others, including children." I had been putting on everyone else's mask personally and professionally, all the while forgetting to put on my own, and I was suffocating. I had to organize a program that would allow me to be the professional school counselor I knew I was intended to be, which spawned my desire to improve and apply for the RAMP award.

The drama and crisis at home and at work continued and actually even increased, but this time I had a strategy to lean into God's calling on my life and realize that I can't do it all, and I don't have to; God's got my back, and I just need to keep the eyes of my heart open and be His arms and hands. Surrendering my professional and personal chaos to God allowed me to get out of His way and to watch Him work in not only my life but in the lives of those around me. This in turn strengthened my faith and even my resolve to be the best professional school counselor I could be.

In order to accomplish all of this, I had to bracket my boundaries in that I no longer would let myself take my work home with me. I prayed on the way home for the students, staff, and families in crisis and let it go once I got home until I picked up the burden the next day when I arrived in my office. I had begun to master the art of "letting go and letting God"—until I met my student Paul. Paul pushed those newfound boundaries both personally and professionally. There was just something special about Paul.

Friday, June 5, 2009, 5:00 p.m.: I found myself sitting in the front row of the middle school auditorium where I was the school counselor. I was holding the hand of a woman, who, like myself, was a Christian single mom with a very limited support system. Although she and I had a lot in common, tonight there was one major difference: she was mourning the loss of her son, and I was the employee who organized his memorial and reception.

Although it was an unusual task that fell under "other duties as assigned," I was honored to be the leader of the celebration of life (although very short), for this amazing young man. One by one, for over three hours, people shared how Paul had touched their lives. I found myself reflecting on Paul, and his influence on me personally and professionally, but also on the other students who had influenced me while alive and continue to do so now that they have died.

My motto was, "If you've got issues, I've got tissues; don't suffer in silence, and friends, don't let friends suffer either." Every student knew it and could recite my mantra without a hitch. Although when repeated it brought a smile, we all knew that this was a very serious subject. As a professional school counselor, I worked in the domain of personal/social/emotional needs of students, but when it came to a student's death, which was always untimely, it didn't seem like there were enough tissues in the world to address the issues we were facing as a school.

Whenever you have so many individuals in one place such as a school, loss is inevitable. Teachers die; parents pass. I held the hand of one single mom who had twin middle schoolers (one of whom had severe autism) the night before she died of pancreatic cancer. The hospital called me at her passing and told me to pick up my new children— that I was, for that moment, at least, their new mom, as they had no family. I got them the help they needed, but I wasn't in a position as a single mom myself to meet their needs at the time. I considered it, and I really wish I could have done it.

One year our nurse was murdered by her husband, who was our PTA president, to get the life insurance money. He was eventually caught. Right before he killed her, he sent her flowers at work, which were on her desk with a card depicting a man coming out of a doghouse. I said, "Lovely flowers," to which she responded, "Hardly enough to make up for what he has done to me." Soon after, she was found dead in her own home after the police had unknowingly stood at her front door while she was being murdered inside. Their son was one of my highest-achieving students, and he lost both parents in one day.

Death is a part of life, and even shocking deaths such as our school nurse's murder can be absorbed, but the death of a child just seems unnatural. I think most people would agree that children are not supposed to die. Professional school counselors do not get enough training, especially on how to process personal grieving while helping others to cope. I was naïve to the fact that having a student of mine die would affect me personally and professionally. Guiding over a thousand people through unexplained loss, grief, bereavement—whatever you want to call it—is a noble calling, but it is also an overwhelming one. Loss can lead to grief, and it is unique for each person. It is multidimensional and requires the professional school counselor or mental health worker to have the competence, confidence, and comfort level to help the hurting move into healing.

Professional school counseling (as is the case with many helping professions) is a field that is filled with legal and ethical guidelines, but the line between who I am as a person and who I am as a professional sometimes becomes blurred more than bracketed as I become enmeshed with the families and lives that I am serving.

One thing is clear: when everyone else is freaking out and shutting down, it is my job to keep everyone calm and carry everyone else on. We render emotional first aid to those that are hurting. Due to the overwhelming need, professional school counselors can at times be immune to feeling in the moment, as there is no time to grieve or process due to the next crisis occurring.

When I took classes in school counseling in graduate school, we learned a lot about psychologist Carl Rogers and his concept of "unconditional positive regard"—basic acceptance of all. As I started to develop my counseling theory, I adopted God's calling upon my life, "unconditional love," as my mantra. Although it is not easy to always show love to every person who comes through my office door, especially when it is an irate teacher or parent using me to vent on, I do believe love is a choice, and one that I have to do my best to make, to fulfill my ministry calling of being a professional school counselor.

When I started in my career, I always told myself that as long as a student didn't want to talk about death, I would be fine. The very first day on the job, the floodgates opened, and it seemed like grief counseling was all I did. Dogs died, grandparents died, relatives died, and the list goes on. I am grateful now for these students and situations, as they required me to get additional professional development in grief counseling, and I went from not being able to talk about death to not being able to stop talking about death. I became the "go to" person when someone experienced loss. Former students even came back to see me when a loss occurred in their lives. I was honored, but overwhelmed.

Loss on a school campus comes in many forms, some not as obvious as others. One day in the spring after a particularly violent gang-related killing spree on the local streets, students and staff were on high alert. Racial tensions were so high you could feel it in the air. Staff awaited the next passing period or lunchtime when students would congregate and violence would ensue. Students were restless; they didn't sleep at night, as they would keep being awakened by gunshots and screeching tires. Everyone was stressed. The walkie-talkie stood dutifully on the counseling secretaries' desk outside my office. Then the call rang forth through the speaker.

"Lockdown—reported active shooter on campus."

A call came in from a ninth-grade classroom on the north side of our 64-acre campus.

"There is someone shooting at us from outside," the student yelled.

The secretary asked, "Where is your teacher?" She was on the floor, not moving. The secretary then realized that the call was from her son's classroom. She had recently announced that she was pregnant, and she went into panic mode in fear for her son's safety.

Turns out it wasn't an active shooter but stressed nerves and imaginations that immediately conjured a shooter after hearing metal shrapnel bombard their window that overlooked a dangerous park. The gardener's metal equipment had flown into pieces and repeatedly hit the classroom window very hard, with an accompanying sound that resembled gunfire. There was loss for those who were present in that they lost their peace of mind, but also for our secretary, who lost her unborn baby due to shock.

The memorial bulletins in my storage box have piled up over the years: a sixth-grade girl in a skateboarding accident, whose popular sister was my student who felt conflicted over feelings of grief and joy as her career as an actress was taking off.

A car accident claimed the lives of two of my high school students. So young, so senseless, so sudden.

One of my students committed suicide. He didn't exhibit any of the "typical textbook" signs, but that didn't stop him from going home and hanging himself in his closet. Suicide should not be glorified, so his story will end as his life did— unexplained and suddenly.

I lost one student to a plane crash; her dad and mom were the pilot and co-pilot, killing the whole family except the sister who was in college and couldn't go on the family vacation.

There was the day when in essence I lost two students at once. In a high-need urban school, race relations sometimes get heated, and gang activity emerges. One of my former students who had been transferred out of our school stabbed one of my ninth graders to death. My high school, as well as the middle school students who were just exiting the building, witnessed the event, and some even tried to save the victim. As an 18-year-old, the perpetrator received the death sentence. Two students' lives over in a heartbeat. Both were victims in a sense of the societal woes that plague our streets. The community still cries out for healing, as do both of their families. As a professional school counselor, I try to stand in the middle and bring healing to broken communities beyond the school walls.

Senseless gun violence continued to disrupt my students' dreams. I had an 11-year-old student who died because of a gunshot wound in the upper torso. Although he was not in a gang, he was a victim of gang violence, and the murderer still runs free to this day. While in the trauma room, his mother begged the doctor to take her heart and give it to her son. Although the surgeon did everything he could, including ripping open his chest cavity and sticking his fingers into his little heart to try to stop the bleeding, the child was gone, and the surgeon wept. He publicly admitted to wanting to quit his career that day. His job was over, but mine was just beginning. Consoling a school of 1,500 middle schoolers was thrust to the top of my ever-growing to-do list. I could totally relate to the surgeon's remarks in that moment, but I knew that it was my calling to help stop the psychological bleeding. Students flooded my office to cry and sign a memorial poster for the family. I was invited to serve on a citywide crisis committee to address gang violence. I put on my "advocate hat," and I was proud to feel that I could in some small way give my student a voice at the table.

Death knows no boundaries. As a professional school counselor in a diverse, urban school district, I have had the opportunity to work with students from all backgrounds, including socioeconomic. Where one mom did not have money to pay the utilities or rent, and certainly not the high cost of burying her son, other students were well off.

Every year as I review state assessment materials, I sit on the auditorium stage to sort and count the tests and I remember a former student of mine who used to sing and perform on that stage. I knew him not only professionally but also personally since his childhood through church. After graduating at 18 years of age, he went off to college on the East Coast to pursue his dreams. Unfortunately, he died from alcohol poisoning because of a freshman fraternity hazing ritual. So very tragic that a young man who was known for making good choices died as a result of one bad one. This event does not define his life, but in this case it ended it.

I had one graduate student die in his early twenties. He was very well liked by his peers, and the faculty. He was a large statured Christian young man who sang like an angel. He had just graduated and was so excited to start his new journey as a professional school counselor. He had a brain aneurism and died suddenly. I attended his memorial service the day after my own mom had died. His dad took to the stage, and in his broken English he said, "My son had a dream. He wanted to go on for his doctorate degree in Education. Who will agree to do this in his honor?" The gym was filled with literally hundreds of people, many of them college aged. I thought, *Well, certainly one of his young friends will take up the torch for him, and get an EdD.* Silence. Crickets. The dad posed the question again through tears and took out his cell phone and video recorded the audience as he made his plea. Still no response. My mom had just died the night before; I couldn't even think straight. Why was I even at this service? I didn't even remember driving there. Nonetheless, I felt compelled to raise my hand. My graduate students in attendance sitting around me gasped, as they knew that I already had a full plate with being a single mom, working a full-time job as a professional school counselor and three part-time jobs as the lead counselor, and teaching at night at two universities. Then out of the corner of my eye, a young girl appeared and gave me a piece of paper and a pen. She wanted me to sign a promissory note that I would fulfill the deceased's dream on his behalf! All eyes were on me. I reluctantly signed, and the crowd applauded. One of my graduate students leaned over to me and queried, "What are you going to give up to make that happen?" To which I replied, "Nothing." The next week I took the entrance exam for the program. I didn't study at all; I hadn't slept in a week as I had just found out that my mom had suffered from paranoid schizophrenia. I had historically been bad at math. I remembered that "c" was the most common answer in a multiple-choice test. I sat for two hours pushing the answer "c" for every math question, not even bothering to read the question. Half-praying I wouldn't do well enough on the test to have to fulfill my promise and for "God to get me a way out of this." Half-praying I would pass so I could make good on my promise and appease the prompting of the Holy Spirit that I know I felt at the memorial service. Turns out I scored higher on math than I did English, a first for me. I was accepted to the program even though their rejection rate was higher than their acceptance rate. The next three years went by in a whirlwind blur. I graduated with an emphasis in school counseling. I had learned even more about what it meant to be a professional school counselor. I kept a picture of my graduate student on my binder. Whenever I felt like I just couldn't handle one more thing, I would gaze at his smile and think of his dad at the memorial. Little did my deceased graduate student know, but God used his death to guide me into pursuing my educational goals. Turns out he was an amazing counselor even post mortem!

Although losing a student to an accident of any kind, suicide, murder, plane crash, or alcohol poisoning are all difficult burdens to bear, no student deaths have struck me as hard as losing students with special needs over the years. One of my favorite students was wheelchair bound. His health degenerated over his high school years. He went from regular education classes to special education classes for the moderate-severe special education population. Unfortunately, he died of heart complications at age 18, the day before he was to be honored at his Catholic church. He had been in a wheelchair since he was six years old. At work, he motivated me to move forward with a smile daily in spite of my circumstances, just as Paul did.

It was the first day of school for Paul and me, him an incoming sixth grader and me serving in my new role of professional school counselor, where I had previously been a special education teacher. I was so nervous. Not only was I in a new profession, but with a brand new principal who was known for her high standards. I dressed for success in my new suit and modest heels. As a special education teacher, my attire had been casually comfortable, with sensible shoes. I was not well versed in the fine art of walking in high heels. Clipboard in hand, complete with paper and writing utensil, I took to the hallways. I didn't know what exactly my mission was, but I figured holding a clipboard made me look official and legitimate. The bell rang, and 1,500 diverse middle schoolers in a large urban school district dashed all around me, desperate to be in class on time for the first day. Over the walkie-talkie, I heard the principal's voice calling for me. She wanted to see me in her office right away. Eager to please, I made a beeline down the hall, through the double doors, and down the cement staircase, when IT happened. I twisted my ankle and fell down the stairs, clipboard and walkie-talkie flying through the air; they landed about a foot away from me at the base of the steps, where I lay stunned, staring up at the sky. Suit ripped, shoe broken, nylons torn, clipboard destroyed, walkie-talkie in pieces, face bright red in embarrassment, I took a deep breath and tried not to cuss or cry in front of all of the students I was there to supposedly help. Some "help" I was going to be. I should have paid the school district for allowing me to be at their school site. The students rapidly parted like the Red Sea.

Then, as I lay looking up, contemplating quitting at the moment, I saw a small brown hand extended to me. The student was young, clearly a new sixth grader. He had an amazing smile and thick, bushy, black hair that was gelled to stand straight up. He helped me up and inquired, "Are you okay?" To which I replied, "What a way to start a first day as your counselor." He shook my hand and said, "I am Paul; it is my first day, too. It looks like you could use a hug." As taboo as utilizing a student restroom instead of a faculty one, as an educator I knew never to hug a student unless the student hugs you; even then, make sure it is a side hug that has no frontal body contact, only side by side with a one-handed tap on the shoulder. He reached up and threw his arm around my shoulders. I thought, *Wow, this is an impressive young man; he even knows about side hugs!*

The adrenaline from the fall started to wear off, and pain was setting in. Choking back tears, I asked, "What is that for?" to which he replied, "For all the great things you are going to do for me and the other students at our school." I raised my arm in "side hug" fashion, but something felt amiss. Paul had no shoulder or left arm! No wonder he was so good at side hugs! I knew then that an angel had touched me. I didn't quit; in fact, it gave me stronger resolve that if this young man can survive junior high, so can I! First lesson from Paul, "When you fall, pick yourself up, brush yourself off, and start all over again," and help someone up who has in some way fallen; let the person know that you believe in him/her.

I went home that day to journal my daily experiences as I always did, and I titled my new journal, for my new chapter in life, "One Armed Hugs, and Other Joys of Counseling." I decided right then that I would journal the impact that my students had on me in a way that I could one day share with other new professional school counselors, all the journeys ahead of them. Although there was a book full of triumphs, I had no idea how many tragedies would also fill those pages. However, from each young person I learned far more than I could have ever taught. Lessons about living and dying that would last a lifetime. However, it is Paul who taught me the most.

One of my first assignments was to organize an annual event called "Disability Awareness Day" in October. Paul had become a regular in my office, always dropping by to greet me, and he probably wanted to make sure I hadn't fallen and knocked myself out in my office. We really hit it off, and we spent a good amount of time daily discussing school and life. He volunteered to help me organize the newly named Ability Awareness Day (thanks to Paul's recommendation to emphasize the positive.) All 500 sixth graders in the school would go around to stations in their PE class to learn about what it feels like to have special needs. I set myself up at a booth about the life of Helen Keller and taught students the sign language alphabet through a bingo game. The purpose was to increase students' appreciation of people with special needs and to promote an anti-bullying climate.

Paul offered to lead a booth regarding loss of limb. I actually had three students in the sixth grade with limb loss at the time. The other two had genetic anomalies. In Paul's case, he had been a typical, healthy child until he was ten years of age, when he was diagnosed with neurofibromatosis and a malignant peripheral nerve sheath tumor, a cancer that required the amputation of his arm and shoulder. Paul had been given a prosthetic, but it never fit him well due to his lack of a shoulder blade, and it inhibited him from doing the things he loved to do. It didn't even match his skin tone, and those around him agreed that he didn't look like himself with it on. Lessons from Paul: keep it real, and be yourself.

To demonstrate to the student body how difficult it would be to have a sudden limb loss, I recommended that Paul lead an activity that would allow participants to color, cut, and paste with one non-dominant hand. I started to make a list and gather the needed supplies. Paul smiled his loving smile and suggested, "How about we just let them try tying their shoes with one hand?" Paul taught me more lessons in that moment: don't overthink things, and keep it simple.

Not surprisingly, Paul's booth was the most popular, and he was undoubtedly the most popular person on campus. He set up shop in his booth annually, even when he was so sick from chemotherapy treatments that he had to keep running to the bathroom. Lesson from Paul: show up.

Through this process, I learned that my students with limb loss needed accommodations and modifications in the classroom setting in order to support their special needs. I called in an expert in the field to help. He met with the students and addressed their concerns. Paul expressed that rapid note taking was a challenge for him as his paper continued to slip all over the desk. The expert handed him a clipboard to try, and Paul was so happy. He jumped up and hugged the man with a big grin on his face and said, "You have changed my life!" Paul certainly knew how to make a person's day. Even with what is commonly referred to as "chemo brain," when a person on chemotherapy suffers from memory loss and cloudy or foggy thoughts, as well as frequent absences due to hospitalizations, he was almost a 4.0 student, but at least now a clipboard would make that accomplishment a little easier for him. More lessons from Paul that would guide me over the years: ask people what they need. Do your best to support them; smile, hug, and say, "Thank you; I appreciate you."

Paul didn't let his health stop him from living life to the fullest. His favorite T-shirt read, "I love life, it is worth the fight." Much like his favorite quote, "I am too positive to be doubtful. Too optimistic to be fearful. And too determined to be defeated."

Paul kept busy in school and out. Every morning he would independently raise the American flag. This was no small feat, as on the days Paul was absent due to hospitalization we had to have two typical students do the task. Paul appreciated all of the medical assistance he was receiving in the United States.

He and his mom had fled the Philippines, leaving Paul's little brother in the care of family to get him the emergency medical care he needed here in the US. They thought he would have the surgery and return to their home soon; this never happened, as Paul needed continued treatments and doctors' appointments. He always felt guilty about his brother having to be left behind and in essence losing his mom for his whole youth. Paul didn't have an outside therapist, and Jean had cancer, so I understood the terms and tests he spoke of; due to this, I was able to gain a unique perspective on this young man's life and struggles as he shared with me over the course of four years.

Paul was also in choir and the choral jazz group. He spoke and sang at fundraisers for the City of Hope and the Ronald McDonald House. There would always be a captivated audience when Paul sang. He would share his story and fill the room with angelic tones. The only other sound was that of people sniffing from crying so hard. Benefactors would pass forward checks for thousands when he hit his final note. Another lesson from Paul: giving money is good, but giving of yourself is greater.

Paul was not only a musician and a scholar, participating in rigorous academic coursework; he was also an amazing athlete. He was skilled at baseball, golfing, badminton, basketball, and sword fighting. (Rumor has it that he literally disarmed eight dual-bladed fighters in a training session one day.) His Facebook quote read, "Singing is my passion. Helping others is a must. I can't leave anyone out to dry. Whether I know you or not, I will lend a helping hand. I play every sport but soccer. I just can't kick!" Lessons from Paul: always be a friend to the friendless, and tenacity is contagious.

Paul also enjoyed being a leader on campus, as he was the Commissioner of Welfare on our student council. He additionally enjoyed acting and dancing, and in true teenaged boy form he was a skilled gamer.

With so much character and talent, it is easy to understand why he won the Most Inspiring Student Award two times. I wrote an article about his accomplishments, and he was featured on the cover of the local newspaper for his heroic efforts in life. More lessons from Paul, just like the Lokai bracelet motto, "When you are at your lowest stay hopeful; when you are at your highest, stay humble."

Paul was given the unique opportunity to be a consultant and extra in the film *My Sister's Keeper*. I cherish my copy of this incredible movie that depicts life from the perspective of a young person with cancer. I always pause the DVD during the scenes where Paul is shown as an extra in chemotherapy, seated by the stars. He was able to view his part in the movie before he passed, and he was so happy to have contributed to people's understanding of how this disease affects so many young people. Not to mention that he got to meet Cameron Diaz. Thanks to the Make a Wish foundation, Paul was able to travel to Disney World, and he had the opportunity to meet Kobe Bryant. Paul felt so fortunate to interact with these superstars, but everyone who knew Paul knew that they were the lucky ones to meet him.

Paul was promoted from middle school to high school, but his health took a turn for the worse, and he was unable to attend high school. He lived across the street from our middle school, and he spent as much time as he could with me at work. His single mom had to work, and he didn't have any family to keep him company, so he spent many hours alone at home very sick. His friends were all in class, and our school was the only school in the US he ever really knew. We were his support system. He had a Home Hospital teacher who stopped by daily to give him his new packets to study, which didn't take him long to devour. As time went on and his cancer progressed, the visits became fewer and further between. The office would buzz with excitement when Paul stepped onto campus. Rushing to meet Paul at my door was the joy of my day. Everyone would chatter, "Have you seen Paul?" "I can't wait to see Paul." "Paul's here!" With every visit, his coloring turned grayer. That unshakable odor of chemo chemicals and death began to emanate more strongly from his every cell.

His beautiful head of thick, black hair had vanished under the spell of chemo treatments to reveal his bald head. He wasn't supposed to be around people in fear that he would contract some contagious disease like a cold, which could prove fatal for him, but as in everything Paul persevered.

Then the call came. Paul's mom informed me that he had once again been hospitalized. I knew in my gut that this time he would not be coming out to once again greet me at my office door.

I drove to the pediatric cancer hospital almost an hour away. I knew that he was in the best of hands. All at no cost to Paul's mom. I vowed that I would always give a donation, however small, when asked to support nonprofit charities. I have stayed true to this vow. Every time I am at the grocery store, movies, or wherever, I thank the requester for the opportunity to give. I have Paul to thank for this new, less Scrooge-like, version of myself, as I have seen firsthand how lives can be changed one dime at a time.

The hospital reeked of death; I knew, as I had smelled it before. It permeates your nostrils, and you can't get it out, even when you leave. It stays with you, haunting your innermost being. I sanitized my hands, put on the medical mask provided, and slipped on the robe and gloves to cover my germ-infested clothes. Paul rallied a smile. His eternal optimism shone through his dimming eyes. As usual, he refused to sleep when he had company; he felt it was disrespectful to a person who had come all that way to visit him. He didn't want to be rude, so I kept my visit short, knowing that he needed rest. His mom had gone home to shower and pack more clothes. Alone we sat in silence. His eyes said it all. No need to speak. It was time to just be. I drove home in a daze. Not sure how I even got home, I couldn't remember the drive. I tried to journal my journey, but I was at a loss for words. I fell asleep while praying.

The next morning at work, Paul's mom called and sounded like she was in a state of shock. She was silent, so I asked her if Paul was okay, but she didn't respond. I followed up with, "Where's Paul?" She whispered, "In heaven."

As the morning went on, I checked my email, and there was one from Paul, very brief, all lower case, thanking me for all that I had done for him. I ran out of tissues on my desk, I cried so hard. This young man had a gift of making every soul feel its worth. This would be my new mission. To make every person I encountered feel his/her value in this world.

The next couple of weeks were filled with a grieving school community. It was the end of the school year, and promotion was fast approaching, our busiest season. This memorial was the culminating event, and I was the final speaker.

"In conclusion, thank you for taking the time today to share in this celebration of Paul's extraordinary life. I have no doubt that those in heaven are standing at the pearly gates excitedly exclaiming, "Have you seen Paul?" "I can't wait to see Paul!" "Paul is here!" and he is greeting them with his warm smile, bushy black hair, and a big, two-armed hug!

I could never list all of his life lessons that Paul bestowed upon me, but here are a few:

1. Be courageous—When you fall, pick yourself up, brush yourself off, and start all over again, and help someone who has fallen and can't get up physically or emotionally
2. Be a person of integrity—Keep it real, and be yourself.
3. Keep it simple—Don't overthink things.
4. Support others—Smile, hug, and say thank you.
5. Give your time, talent, and treasure—Giving of your money is good, but giving of yourself is greater.
6. The Lokai Principle—When you are at your lowest, stay hopeful; when you are at your highest, stay humble.

3.
Maybeth's Box

It is February 2, Groundhog Day, my deceased best friend's birthday, and my mother's death date, and all I see are shadows. It is going to be a long winter. Long winters were something I was used to, having been raised in Minnesota.

The year is 1976, and the temperature is 7 degrees in Minneapolis, not factoring in windchill. I am seven years old, it is five in the morning, and my single mom is outside unplugging the car, a daily ritual to protect the engine from freezing temps, pouring hot water on the windshield prior to scrubbing off the ice that accumulated as she warmed up the car, spreading salt in the driveway, and shoveling us out so she can get to her job as a secretary by 9:00 a.m. sharp. You would think she was gearing up for a long commute, but she worked only a few blocks away from our house. She had to take me to my grandma's house, where I would stay until time to walk to school, and then she would drive all the way back to her place of employment. Many nights I just stayed with my grandma, as it was such a hassle to get me there in the morning. As for me, I stumbled out of bed, eyes still closed, bare feet freezing on the linoleum floor of my attic bedroom with no heat. I walked downstairs and stood in front of the heater in my nightgown, putting on my underwear backward as I was prone to do, dressing myself in the dark with my eyes closed. I envisioned myself walking the distance in my red snowsuit to my school, where kids would ask me repeatedly why I didn't have a dad.

I did see my dad that morning, however. He snuck out the garage back door as my mom opened the front garage door to access the car. I had been looking out the window and saw a man in the shadows, heading down the block. My dad was homeless, due to his refusing to work and insisting on spending his life in a drunken stupor. My parents divorced when I was two due to his domestic violence, and he made it a habit of randomly and periodically showing up from California uninvited. This time he didn't leave before the snow arrived, so our garage became his part-time nighttime dwelling.

No time for breakfast. My mom yelled for me to hurry up and get in the car. We both got in, me sitting behind her, our breath billowing white before us. A loud noise came upon us; the snowplow. It was helpful for accessing the streets but left high piles of snow in its wake that blocked our newly cleared driveway. My mom made a moaning sound and started to exit the car to re-shovel the driveway. I grabbed the doorjamb to pull myself up and lean forward to yell to her to be careful because I had just seen dad leaving the garage where he had slept the night before. She unknowingly slammed the car door on my left hand. I screamed in pain. She couldn't hear me. I wailed, writhing, until she returned. I tried to focus on the snow-buried rose bushes that I could see through the garage window. My mom loved roses, especially yellow ones. She would say, "Life is not a bed of roses." At seven, I hadn't totally grasped what she meant by that, but now I was starting to get the gist.

She returned, and I told her what happened. She said it was dumb to put my hand in the car door, and she handed me a snowball and told me to squeeze it, so my hand would freeze and I wouldn't feel the pain.

We carried on to my grandma's house. There wasn't a soul on the road. She couldn't access my grandma's street due to the plow not having made its way through yet, so she told me to get out and walk to her house. Off I went in the freezing cold. The snowdrifts were so high I couldn't even see the houses lining the street. I kept falling in the snow banks. Then I heard the voice of my grandma yelling, "Bobbi, follow my voice!" She had my mom late in life and was morbidly obese and barely mobile, so she couldn't come after me. I did press on to be greeted with warm oatmeal and hot black coffee to dip my chunky peanut butter toast into. She kissed my throbbing hand. I had survived yet another Minnesota morning with my mom. I would stay at Grandma's and have my usual Swedish meatball TV dinner in front of *Sesame Street*; life was good.

My mom loved to watch TV, and we did so at night before bed whenever I was with her. In November of 1976, when I was eight, my mom decided that we would watch the movie *Sybil* together, so I would appreciate what a good mom I had. I didn't really need to be traumatized by that movie to know that I did have a good mom. Little did I know that, at such a tender age, I was developing grit, resilience, and faith that would carry me throughout the seasons of life, through the blizzards and tornadoes that would plague my daily existence.

My mom's box is a tough one to empty; it contains photos, her poems, the book and musical she self-published, and her journal of the 19 months of torture she experienced prior to her death, along with letters addressed to my dad that I recovered from my dad's storage when he died; they tell of a woman abused, begging for mercy from his hand. She never once told me about this chapter of her life—or any chapter, for that matter. I am continually trying to put pieces of this mysterious puzzle together, and I will share what I know.

My favorite item in her box is a photo album that has a quote by the British playwright James M. Barrie: "God gave us memory, so that we might have roses in December." Inside it are pictures I recovered of my maternal grandparents. My grandma showed up one day with my grandpa and announced to her two children from a previous marriage, "This is your new dad." Years later, she announced that she was going out, and she returned to declare to the same two children, "This is your new sister." They didn't even know that she had been pregnant. This was how this family functioned.

My grandmother had a strong work ethic, and my grandfather was an inventor of items that were patented and sold, including an under-pressure faucet and valve tool (a gas pump) and furnace cleaner. He was an alcoholic who stopped drinking the day my mom was born. I remember fondly creating inventions with him in the garage from various pieces of scrap metal that he kept. My grandpa died when I was seven. He told me before he died of throat cancer, through his raspy voice, that he was proud of me, and thought I would make a great waitress someday. My grandmother died when I was 13. My great aunt Alice had taken over my primary care after the death of my grandpa, as my grandmother was unable.

Pictures of my mom in her younger years include one from the time when my mom turned 18 and she and her friend were supposed to move to California together to satisfy their wanderlust. Her best friend committed suicide the night before they were to leave, and my mom got up and left for San Francisco on her own.

She moved to a small apartment near the corner of Haight and Ashbury in 1960. She was the opposite of a hippie; she likened herself to having been more like a Jacqueline Kennedy. She was a secretary for the IRS and wore suits. Not long after she arrived she caught a very serious case of the flu and probably should have been hospitalized, but she refused medical attention. She was all alone in a big city and lying on the living room floor thinking she was going to die alone. A delivery boy arrived at her door and gave her a dozen yellow roses sent from her new coworker. She felt then that she would survive and that someone cared whether she lived or died, and she was going to be okay. Ever since then, yellow roses gave her confidence and comfort.

Although she did not come from a family of faith, she had walked herself to church down the block every Sunday since she was 13 years old. She was active in her local church in San Francisco and never missed a Sunday there either. One day in 1967, the young adult group of which she was a member handed out coffee to the homeless. My mom invited my transient dad to come in for a visit with the young adult group and warm up with a cup of coffee. From that time on, they went on picnics, and he always brought alcohol even though my mom didn't drink. She had him and a couple of friends over for dinner. He walked in as if he owned the place, sat down in the living room and turned on the TV, and spoke to the couple as if they were the first time visitors, not him. They had some good times together exploring San Francisco when he wasn't drunk, but usually he was. Four months later, she asked him when he was going to ask her to marry him; he said, "Okay, I will marry you"; and that is what they did right away in Reno, Nevada, in a courthouse. She felt that he was handsome, intellectual, and had great potential if she could clean him up and get him to stop drinking. He thought she had a smile that could light up a room and an infectious laugh. She also had been depressed for three months prior due to a breakup with a previous boyfriend, who apparently went on to invent neon for glow-in-the-dark jewelry. My mom had wanted to be a social worker and loved to save people, but none of that ever panned out. My dad frequented the local bars and brought home strange men and women to the apartment while my mom was in the bedroom waiting up for him. He was well known amongst the promiscuous women and gay men of the neighborhood.

Six weeks into their marriage, my mom started writing my dad notes and letters to communicate with him, as she was at work all day and he was out all night. This was also a safer way to share her feelings with him. These letters were recovered from his storage unit after his death, and my mom never made mention of the hell she survived. Growing up, whenever I asked about my dad, she would say, "Hurt people hurt people. He is an alcoholic, a very sick individual who needs your love and prayers." Over the years, that is what I extended. It is probably for the best that these letters weren't recovered earlier; he would have received neither from me, knowing what he had done to my mom and, by extension, to me.

At age 24, six weeks after they had wed, she wrote, "Another thing that has ruined me is never going to church on Sunday. I love church. God means a great deal to me. I have temporarily lost God, but I must find Him again before my entire life falls apart." She went on to say that my dad would stagger late into church, sit in the front next to the pastor's wife, and breathe his alcohol odor all over her, as he squirmed and nearly fell out of the pew; then he would get up, go to the bathroom to drink, and do it all over again. The pastor's wife, who was my mom's friend, warned her that he was an alcoholic, and to be careful and protect herself.

Prior to their marriage, he would show up at my mom's apartment in the middle of the night, drunk, making a loud scene accusing her of having men with her—there were none. She would let him in to quiet him down, and he would pass out on her living room floor. Yet, she married him.

Her next letter to him, "If I am not pregnant now, which I very well may be, I will begin taking birth control pills to prevent a child from suffering in this household. He would be frightened to death of you." At 24, she was pregnant with me, and he continued to get drunk and be violent with her. She wrote, "I have lost any kind of feeling. It has been drawn from me like a magnet. Like sap draining from a tree. It is not as if I never had it. It has been pulled from me. I no longer care about anything. I have no interests at all. I am dead. I know who has done this to me. A man who is unable to communicate in anything but a roar; a man who is nasty in mind and body; a man who has had no love in his life; a man who enjoys yelling at people; a killer."

In another excerpt, "Then came along the killer. He frightened me when he came home after drinking heavily; frightened me to a point of no return, and I am still frightened of him. He slaps me around freely, without even an apology afterwards. He feels there is nothing wrong in brutality."

54

I was born on Sunday, July 28, 1968, in Oakland. My dad was not present; he had been out drinking the night before. My mom was alone in the delivery room. She checked into the hospital to have me (her one and only interaction with the medical profession in her lifetime) and then demanded to be released immediately afterward. She called my dad and let him know that I was born, and that she expected roses. It was a Sunday; he said no flower shop was open. She never got her roses, but she dressed me in yellow.

Twelve weeks later, she wrote to my dad, "Bobbi has gone through a great deal these last few months. She has become aware of what is going on around her. You just don't hide hate. Isn't it too bad an innocent child had to become involved? I am so sorry she was born, for her sake."

She spelled my name differently in every letter, from Bobby to Bobbie to Bobbi. In any form my name means, "Excellent worth, shining with fame." My life verse is Philippians 4:13: "I can do all things through him who gives me strength." Although all very appropriate, I highly doubt she was aware of any of this when she named me. She said I was named after a homecoming queen whom she admired. My dad said that I was named after his childhood friend. Her life was so filled with chaos and upheaval that a formerly strong, decisive woman couldn't even decide how to spell her own daughter's name.

The domestic violence continued to take its typical cyclical course—tension building, acute violence, reconciliation/honeymoon, calm, . . . and it all starts over again. However, it seemed that in my parent's case the reconciliation/honeymoon and calm might only last a matter of hours while my dad slept off his hangover, and then abruptly back to tension and acute violence. My mom would write letters of apology for her being the cause of his drinking and beating her. She was all alone; her family knew nothing, thinking she was a strong, happily married new mom in California. She had to let all social outlets go, including church and friends and had to frequently miss work, which she hated to do, as work was a source of pride for her.

She wrote to him, "I haven't a husband because he has beat me in every way possible to an absolute pulp. I have given up loving my parents, and the people around me. I have no love in my heart. It is gone. I have been killed. I live in emptiness."

After a year, she had suffered enough physical (being beaten), verbal/emotional (being threatened), mental/psychological (being bullied), financial/economic (being taken advantage of—he didn't work but took all of her earnings to buy alcohol and gifts for other women), and spiritual abuse (being forbidden to attend church) that she cashed out her retirement savings, and they relocated to San Diego for a fresh start. My dad was to go to college, and my mom would work to support them.

Immediately he started drinking at the local bars, never enrolled in school, and the abuse continued and increased. This went on for almost a year, and then my mom left for Minnesota, the land of 10,000 lakes, one million mosquitos, and a family who loved her and wanted her (and me) home. My dad followed, and it got harder to conceal the truth from the family. My mom felt a renewed sense of power and strength knowing that her mom and dad, although elderly, lived close by, and she repeatedly kicked my dad out of the house. She finally had the home turf advantage.

The last night I remember her letting him in, he was pounding down the door demanding to be let inside the little one-bedroom house my mom had bought with her work savings. I was asleep in bed. My mom kept yelling for me to come to her. I was so sleepy and scared. I was about three years old, and it was the middle of the night. I heard her scream, followed by a thump and silence. I ran to the kitchen. My dad had hit my mom; he had backed her up against the refrigerator and struck her in the head.

The back of her head had caught on the edge of the metal freezer door handle and was bleeding profusely, but, as usual, she would not get medical help. I stood in front of her, crying, pleading for my dad to stop. He had never hit me as far back as I could remember. He charged into the back door entryway. He took my mom's prized possession, a ceramic Cinderella carriage statuette that my grandpa had given her when she graduated from high school. I knew it was the one thing in the house I was not allowed to touch. He threw it down the cement stairs. Surprisingly, only one of the horse's heads broke off. I ran to retrieve it, trying desperately to make the horse's head reattach. My mom stumbled into the living room and sat on the couch crying, holding her head. I tried to console her.

My dad went to the bed that my mom and I shared and fell asleep. My mom asked me why I didn't come when called and told me that I was late, and it was my fault that she would now go blind from the big lump that was forming on the back of her head. It was my fault that my mom would be blind. I would never again disobey, and I would always come right away when called, sleepy, scared, or not. I was never going to let this happen to my mom again. It was up to me to protect us. I decided right then that from that point out I would be the perfect daughter. I told my grandparents the next morning. They helped my mom take him to court. My dad never entered the house again after that night, and he made plans to go back to California. My mom's physical wounds healed, but the emotional scars remained throughout her lifetime.

My mom continued to write my dad in California with updates regarding how I was doing in early elementary school. She had settled on a spelling of my name and wrote, "Bobbi is not a whiz by any means." She put me in dance lessons because I was so clumsy. He continued to hitchhike back and forth from California to Minnesota, over my early elementary years, but life started to take on a new normal in his absence. A much quieter, happier existence when he wasn't around. For my mom and me, life went on.

It was time for me to start preschool, and I was so excited. Being an only child, and having no cousins, or anyone around my age, proved a lonely existence. My grandparents were elderly and couldn't play with me. I begged to go to preschool, as there was one down the block from our house that had such fun decorations in the window I longed to go there and play with the other children. My mom took me for a visit, and I was hopeful. They had so many toys! The director said that I would need immunizations to start, and my mom said no and told me we were leaving. The director turned to me and asked, "You don't mind getting a shot so you can come to school, do you?" I replied, "No, I don't mind." My mom shot me a disapproving glare. She said that I would not be going to any doctors, or getting any shots—that I would learn at home. Thus ended my preschool career. I spent the next two years playing school with my dolls. I was always the teacher. I stayed with my grandmother, who got me some worksheets from a teacher friend so I could teach myself to read and write.

It was time to start kindergarten, and my grandma and great aunt decided I was going to school. My grandma told me of a time when a doctor had to make a house call for my sick mom when she was a little girl. She hid under the bed and kicked the doctor so hard that he left. She went untreated. They never attempted to get her medical care again in her life, they were so embarrassed. She didn't want me to embarrass her at the doctor, and I didn't. I even got a fun Band Aid and, as always, chocolate chip cookies from Grandma and a York Peppermint Pattie from my grandpa for being good.

We had back-to-school day for parents at kindergarten. My mom was working, and I was the only child without a parent present. We had to read sight words. I couldn't read the word "Who," and the other children looked at me in disgust. Then we had to read instructions to color a workbook page, and I colored all of my items the wrong color, and the kids made fun of me. We sat down on the reading rug to listen to a story and answer questions, and, sad that my parents weren't there, I started to innocently play with a plastic piece on the wall next to me, at which the teacher flipped out and brought attention to my foolishness—sticking my finger in the electrical socket—and the other students rolled their eyes at me. I was in time out, the class dunce, and it was only week one of my educational career.

I spent most of my days and nights living with my grandma and grandpa and visiting my great aunt. I slept on the couch at both places. On Saturdays, my mom would pick me up and take me to dance class, followed by Burger King, and then the laundromat, where I did my own laundry from the day I could reach the top of the machine.

We ran errands and did chores when we were together. Once, while I waited in the car at the bank, a truck pulled up in the parking spot next to me. The occupants had their windows rolled down, as did our car due to the Minnesota humidity and her not wanting to leave the car on with me in it. She gave me strict instructions to stay in the car. The driver and passenger were two males in their late teens. They were laughing and carrying on in a way that made me think they were drunk. Then one said to the other, "Hunting time!" He pulled out a hunting rifle and aimed it at me. My ears burned and stung as I looked down the barrel of the gun. I felt tingly all over, and I froze like a deer in headlights. The passenger laughed and grabbed the gun to admire it. When my mom returned, she said, "Are you feeling okay? You look like you just saw a ghost." I told her what had happened as I cried and shook. She responded, "Nonsense—you saw guys playing with a pool stick, I am sure you were never in danger. Let's go get our Happy Meal."

One day we went to the post office together. As we were standing in line, she noticed the "Most Wanted" posters hanging on the bulletin board. We were standing in a long line. She approached the board and began looking through piles upon piles of listings. Everyone was staring at her. She looked like she was on a mission. She turned to the line of people whose jaws were gaping, and she announced, "You never know when you will see someone you know!" Followed by her smile that could light up a room and light-hearted laugh. Two qualities that I rarely got a glimpse of. When we got to the car, she told me, "Your dad has been involved in bank fraud. I thought I would see him on a poster, and we need the reward money. Time for our nightly Happy Meal at McDonald's."

My mom did cook one time. She made a cake for a work gathering. She was trying to impress the engineers that she worked for. She used red and white icing that melted due to her putting it on the cake before it cooled. She asked me what I thought of it. Being eight, I said that I would just blend the two colors together and make pink frosting. She mixed the icing with a knife. She was so angry; she said she couldn't take such an ugly cake to work. My favorite color was pink; I thought it was pretty. Our house had never smelled like cake before, and it never did again.

The only hobby my mom had was that she liked to go out dancing on Friday and Saturday nights, so I didn't see a lot of her on the weekends. One day she decided that I was overweight—although in hindsight, I was not; it was she who had struggled with her weight her entire life; my grandma and great-grandma also had weight issues. She put us both on a yogurt only diet. She still had to drink her Folgers coffee, however. She was mad that I was six years old and wore a size 6X. She didn't take into consideration that I was a good head taller than the other girls in my class, as well as broad shouldered, thanks to my Norwegian blood.

She wanted me to be a supermodel and starring actress. She entered me in the local Junior Miss pageant. She was disappointed that the name of the winner would be drawn from a hat, but I was relieved. The yogurt diet had worked, although I hadn't been overweight to begin with. My grandmother started sneaking me chocolate chip cookies because she was worried I was too skinny. Her favorite store-bought treat to give me was Little Debbie brownies. One of the nuts made a hole in my molar, and I had a huge, painful cavity. My grandma and great-aunt whisked me off to the dentist. He said I was definitely going to need braces in the near future to address the huge gap between my two front teeth. I looked like a Minnesota gopher. I told my mom, and she said, "Nonsense. Fix them yourself."

"How?"

"Push them together with your fingers until the gums bleed every moment you can." Thereafter, I did. Sitting in school, watching TV, my right thumb and forefinger were like a vice. Within the year my two front teeth touched, and I no longer looked like the University of Minnesota mascot. Braces averted.

Thankfully, I had a relatively healthy childhood. I was prone to serious allergies, however. When I was four, I had a serious earache due to a bad ear infection that almost burst my eardrum. My mom wouldn't take me to the doctor, so my grandpa begged the doctor on my behalf for eardrops. He actually saved my hearing.

I had the chicken pox in third grade. My grandma was my caretaker. My mom stopped by to say, "Don't scratch or you will get scars, and don't you dare let Grandma catch your chicken pox. If she does, she will die, and it will be your fault, and then what will you do?" My grandma tried to feed and care for me, but I tried very hard to stay away from her in fear of killing her. We both survived.

It was the early seventies in a small suburb in the Midwest, with me having only a mom, and no dad. Divorce and single parents were rare in that area at that time. My mom was always busy working or with household chores. She never once read to me. As an only child, I had to keep myself company. I waited for my grandmother once at the dentist office, and there was a copy of *Highlights Kids* magazine. I asked my grandma my address and sent the postcard in on my own, requesting a subscription. Not long after a woman showed up at our house and thanked my mom for requesting more information about the magazine. My mom denied involvement and figured out what I had done. She turned the woman away. No magazines for me. The saleswoman felt so sorry for me she gave me a page of happy face stickers. I loved to read books, including *Winnie the Pooh*. I really identified with the character Tigger, as he was the only one of his kind, and he lived in a world with Rabbit, who was one of many like himself. Over the years, I too would learn how to embrace my Tigger-hood and be proud that I was "the only one," and not just one in a crowd like Rabbit. I learned to love being different from the rest. Both of my parents were an only child, so I had no extended relatives either; I was a rare breed.

Much like my magazine subscription attempt, I filled out the card for the Columbia House records subscription for a penny. I taped the penny to the postcard and gave it to the mail carrier to deliver for me. Sure enough, a dozen records showed up, including the Beach Boys, Captain and Tennille, Sonny and Cher, etc. Then the bill arrived. My mom figured it out right away. She wrote them a letter saying that a minor had made the request, and they couldn't hold me to the contract. They let me keep the records. I had a new best friend, music.

The local firefighters visited our elementary school for an assembly about how to be fire safe at home. The chief said, "Kids, tell your dad that you need an escape ladder if you have a bedroom on the second floor." My ears perked up, then burned. I was SO mad that he said that I needed to tell my dad. My dad had been missing for a long time, and my mom said to just assume he was dead; then my feelings wouldn't be hurt, and if he ever showed up alive, I would be happy that he was still alive.

I waited to meet the firefighter after the assembly, and I blurted out, "What if you don't have a dad?" He said, "Then tell your grandpa." Wrong answer—mine had just died. I walked away under my teacher's disapproving gaze. I went home and told my mom what had happened. She marched me upstairs to my bedroom, swung open the window, and told me to climb out to the tiny ledge on the roof that was about two feet by two feet. I did, and she said, "You don't need a dad, a grandpa, or even a ladder; just jump when the firefighters tell you to. Problem solved!"

I thought she was right: I didn't need a dad. We were strong, in-dependent females. At my great aunt's insistence, I had a few moles removed from under my arm and the back of my neck for cosmetic purposes when I was 14. I knew my Mom approved only because she wanted me to be a model. She dropped me off in the doctor's parking lot. The nurse queried, "Where is your parent?"

"She left."

The nurse's face showed her disgust. Afterward, my mom pulled up into the parking lot, threw me a store-bought sandwich, and took me to musical practice, where I was the lead dancer. As I exited the car, she said, "You good?" I replied, "You betcha." Off she drove. That was my last encounter with the medical profession.

My mom was my Sunday school teacher. I loved Sundays because we always got to spend time together and go to church. She never let me turn the film projector wheel, or pass out papers, or win the prizes that we had bought for the students the weekend before, but I loved it anyway. When I got older, I got to be the helper in her class of younger students. My mom's dream was to marry a pastor, as she desired to be a full-time pastor's wife. Then one day she announced that she was going to direct the children's musical at church. She had no musical knowledge or training, unlike my grandma, who had perfect pitch and could play anything on the piano by ear. She set off to direct the big show, and I was going to have a solo. I practiced my solo for weeks on end, singing it wherever I went. I loved music and singing, and I was so excited! The rehearsals were going great. It was a large cast. Then about one week prior to the show, my mom canceled it and said that she didn't feel like doing it anymore. No explanation to the cast, to me, or to the other adults working on it; she pulled the plug on a great show, much to the disappointment of many—especially me. The next week the assistant pastor announced that he was going to marry a woman from outside the church.

I never once saw my mom pray, read the Bible, or discuss matters of faith outside of Sunday school, but I knew that God was important to her. I don't recall ever being hugged, or told that I was loved, but just as with her relationship with God, I knew her love for me was existent but unspoken.

I had two birthday parties in my youth. One was when I turned eight years old. I got to have a picnic with five of my friends at the local park. We had Kentucky Fried Chicken and clown ice cream cones from Baskin-Robbins with cake. They only had five clown ice cream cones and one more broken one. My mom said, "We'll take it. She will have the broken one." The teenager behind the counter tried to give its hat a frosting fix. We were late, and the clowns were melting fast in the humid, July sun in Minnesota. It was almost 100 degrees outside. She told me to jump in the car and hold the clowns. In our haste, I forgot that the cake was on my seat, and I sat on my cake, but at least we ate melted clowns with brightly colored frosting dissolving everywhere. I got two presents, a broken ceramic coin bank and a big leaky jug of Mr. Bubble bubble bath that spilled all over and left a slippery slime on everything. My mom even took a rare photo. She loved me! I had never been happier. It was official. I had a birthday party!

When I was eight, my mom made me a witch costume for Halloween. I didn't ask to be a witch; I wanted to be an angel like my mom had been in her youth. She also called me "pumpkin," even though I wanted to be called "princess" like my friends' dads called them. I had to settle for a nickname that likened me to a fat, orange gourd. Moreover, for a mask with a giant green nose with a wart on it.

Around this same time, my mom decided that we needed a black cat. He was my first pet. My mom named him Skeezix—I have no idea why. I remember going to pick him up. My mom said to the guy selling him, "Is it a boy or a girl?" He flipped him over, and said, "Well, let's see," with a shy smile on his face. He said, "A boy." My mom said, "Fine, we will take him." When we got to the car, I asked her how he could tell if it was a boy or a girl, and she said replied, "He just could." I felt like that man must have had some magical cat powers or something to be able to flip an animal and tell its gender. I wanted to have those magical powers as well. That was the first and last sex talk we ever had.

Not long afterward I woke up one day to see my mom's leg bleeding from the knee to the ankle, all over her pantyhose. In horror I asked what happened; she said, "The cat attacked me." I asked her if she was going to go to the doctor as the wound looked deep, her skin was hanging, and it was bleeding profusely. I thought she needed stitches. She said, "Nonsense. I am mad that I will have to buy a new pair of pantyhose. I can't be late for work—get in the car." I have no idea why Skeezix did this, but I do know that my mom dripped blood everywhere, even in the white snow. She was clearly in a lot of pain, but she didn't want me to know it. A car hit Skeezix when I was nine years old. My mom sent me into the middle of the street to identify him while she stayed inside. I begged her to not have to look at him. She said he was mine, and I had to do it. I will never forget the image of him lying there. My mom said the neighbor woman had been drinking and was driving home too fast. That was the end of our black cat.

Around the same time, she purchased a Ouija board, and we played it together. It told my mom that she and I would travel across country to California by car together when I was young. She was perplexed by this. I told my grandma what the Ouija board said. My grandma, who was not a Christian, and rather opposed to the Christian faith (but allowed my mom to attend church on her own), told my mom to throw that board away immediately, as it was the devil's tool. I think my grandma was more concerned that the board made it sound like my mom and I would be leaving soon than the fact that she had me play with it.

We moved around a lot, but we didn't leave Minnesota at that time. My mom met a man who was about 15 years her senior. He had an intellectual disability and a second-grade education. He was a punch press operator in a factory. He had self-amputated three of his fingers in his machine, one each on three different occasions. He had adopted a son with his previous wife who had died of cancer.

On the way to their wedding, our car broke down in a very rural part of Iowa. This should have been a red flag that this union should never have happened, but it did. I was nine years old, and now my mom, in essence, had three kids. It just so happened that one was a lot older in years than she was. My mom married him because my grandpa had just died, and she was afraid of my dad, who kept showing up from California. She also really wanted to help his wayward son who was five years my elder. Additionally, I think she was tired of the stigma of being a divorced single mom.

We traveled as a family to Florida to celebrate our new phase of life. My mom loved to travel and had wanted to experience it with me.

My stepdad had a terrible fear of flight. He took many prescription sedatives prior to boarding. The second we got on the plane, he started drinking to calm his nerves. He wasn't typically a drinker, which is one thing my mom really liked about him. The plane before us had to do an emergency landing at the airport due to hurricane-like conditions. Our plane ride started with heavy turbulence, to the point that the flight attendants and everything in the plane were being thrown around, and the passengers were yelling. None were as loud as my stepdad, however, who ran up and down the aisles screaming, "We're all gonna die! We're all gonna die!" I asked my mom if we were going to die, and she said, "No, just pray that we don't, and that it is not someone else's time to go," and that gave me some peace. I remember praying for God to save us. Even the flight attendants were panicked. My stepdad had to be restrained, but that didn't keep him from screaming. Once we safely landed, we checked in to our hotel.

My stepdad fell asleep, and he snored so loudly no one else could sleep a wink. We heard loud noises in the hallway and people screaming, but we thought it was partiers. My stepdad, who had slept very well from all the sedatives and alcohol he had consumed, got up very early, and the police grabbed him and took him to the sand, as we were staying at a hotel on the beach. They told him that there was a bomb scare at all of the hotels on the strip. All of the hotels had been evacuated, but apparently they had missed our room. He ran to get us, screaming as he went, "We're all gonna die! We're all gonna die!" We jumped up, and my mom put on lipstick. We ran for the elevator. It stopped, and opened between floors. I had to be pulled out, and then we ran down what felt like a million flights of stairs. The FBI met us at the exit and took us to duck behind the patrol car parked on the beach. I am not a fan of water, especially in the dark; I turned around and saw a man holding on to a buoy about 100 feet out in the water, dressed in all black, laughing. I told the officer, but he kept telling me to be quiet. Turns out it was the bad guy. The hotel workers had been on strike and wanted to cause the hotel managers problems. The man on the buoy was arrested for placing the bomb threat.

Little did I know that this was just the beginning of a long, challenging five years in my stepdad's home, where I suffered ongoing emotional and sexual abuse, unbeknownst to my mother. Whenever I asked her why she had married him, her response was, "He is a good dancer, and his son needs a mom."

My stepbrother had darker skin than me, brown eyes, and brown hair. One night I woke up to the neighbors yelling. My mom was already up at the front door. Someone had used bleach to write "SPIC" on our front yard grass in huge letters. There was also a cross burning between our house and the neighbors'. They had darker complexions as well. I didn't understand what was happening. There was a lot of screaming going on at the neighbors' house as they worked to put out the fiery cross. My mom said that "SPIC" was a bad word referring to people who were Hispanic. It was hate speech. The bad guys had done this because they thought my stepbrother was Hispanic. Turns out he wasn't; he had a little Native American blood in him, which made more sense to me, as the only thing I had been exposed to that was Mexican was one Taco Bell. "SPIC" remained engrained in our yard and in my mind for a very long time.

Turns out my stepbrother didn't really have a fan club due to his drug involvement. One night I was freezing in my room, more than usual. I noticed that my white window shade had bloody fingerprints on it. The windowpane had been broken. On closer inspection, I realized that there was blood all over my door. A teenager who knew our home well had robbed us. I was terrified to stay home alone after that incident. During this time, the marriage deteriorated, and my stepdad left my mom for another woman. I thought, "Who would want him?"

We left everything and moved out. We drove our beater car to Washington, DC, to live for three days. We had nowhere to live and literally only the shirts on our backs. It was freezing there. I woke up on the third day to find my mom staring out the window. She told me to get up, that we were moving back to Minnesota, to my stepdad's house until we could pull together enough money to move to California. She had moved to the East Coast to get as far away as she could from my dad and stepdad; now we were going to move to the West Coast. She told me that we would not be telling my dad that we made the move, and we were to make him think we still lived in Minnesota for our safety.

Unannounced, we arrived back at my stepdad's house, and she told me to walk in first and proclaim our arrival, which was met with shock. I remember her telling my stepdad that it wouldn't be for long, but it was way too long as far as I was concerned. Eventually, we moved into a low-income apartment, filled with mice everywhere.

I babysat every child in the complex and was doing quite well. My mom continued to work hard and often. She was a secretary by day and worked retail by night. She didn't attend my school functions until my junior year of high school, even though I was frequently the star of vocal, instrumental, and dance performances, as well as plays and musicals. I did all the cleaning, grocery shopping (she gave me $40 a week for everything we needed, so I became very astute at cutting coupons), laundering, feeding myself, babysitting, attending church during the week, doing daily devotionals, practicing my flute, working (I started my first real job at age 15 at a neighboring retail store), and excelling in school. I wanted to be as low maintenance as possible and be the best daughter ever.

One night when I was 14, as my mom was coming home from her second job, I heard a scream outside our apartment door. It was my mom being attacked by a large man in a tattered, beige, Members Only jacket, dirty jeans, and with a black pick in his hair. I watched through the peephole as he violently threw her down the steps. She clutched tightly to her purse and wouldn't let it go. The man struck her, took the purse, and ran off. I froze in shock. I couldn't decide if I should try to run out and help her or call the police, and I couldn't move as I watched the whole situation unfold. It was as if I were three years old all over again. I froze in fear, and my mom suffered at another's hand because I was afraid. I opened the door after the man fled, and she stumbled into the apartment. She was more upset that the man had stolen two silver dollars her dad had given her in her youth than about the physical pain. She had intended to try to sell those coins for money for food; they were all we had. I had failed again as a daughter to protect my mother by letting fear dictate my actions.

The next morning, we were taking out the trash, and the man in the same jacket and pants was at the trashcans next to us. My mom and I hurried to our car, and we both looked at each other and said, "That's him!" He was our new neighbor. I stayed home alone most of the time and didn't feel safe. The mice were out of control, even on the bed at night. We had no money for rent; my mom did not believe in taking handouts or assistance from anyone at any time, but she did relent and allowed us to return to my stepdad's house. Again, it was to be for a short period, but in my mind it went on forever. I would sit staring out the back window of the house crying for hours and praying to God to be my Father and rescue me from that house, and He eventually did.

My mom still felt that the fastest way for us to get money and move out was to have me make money as a model and actress. I enjoyed the performing arts, so I didn't mind. It was imperative to her that we work out at the local women's gym together every single day, no matter what.

Minnesota had a terrible blizzard, and we had a snow day like no other. She insisted that we walk the two and a half miles to the gym to work out. I had plastic boots and a lightweight jacket as the warmest items in my wardrobe. We set out on our mission. It was freezing, and the snow was blinding. Hours later, we reached the gym, and, of course, it was closed, as was everything in the entire city. Not a person to be seen. I almost cried; I had lost feeling in my toes.

I prayed that God would deliver a guardian angel to see us home, and He did. There was no bus service, but as we were walking home a city bus appeared in the midst of the blizzard. It stopped, and we piled on. The bus driver was a female about my mother's age. There was no one on the bus but her. She had taken the bus out to rescue people; there was no public bus service that day. The bus driver yelled at my mom and called her an unfit parent, and it was obvious to her that I was suffering with frostbite.

As my toes started to thaw in the bus, the pain was excruciating as feeling began to return. The nerves in my toes were firing off so hard that I thought I would faint. My mom just kept repeating that I was tough and would be fine. The bus got us as close as possible, and we would need to walk the last half a mile or so. We finally arrived home, and my stepdad, who couldn't care less about me and literally had the sense of a five-year-old, yelled at my mom for hours about how she had almost killed both of us. Her response to my silence was the title from the 1970s song by Lynn Anderson, "I beg your pardon, I never promised you a rose garden." To which she added, "At least we got our exercise."

My grandmother died when I was 13 years old, and my mom and I moved once again into an apartment, although this one was supposedly safer than the last. It was newer, and didn't have mice—only men. One day while I was getting my dinner out of the vending machine downstairs, a middle-aged man pinched my rear end hard. I was 15, and terrified at the event. I ran for the elevator back up to our apartment. When my mom got home from her second job late that night, I told her what had happened, and she told me I must have imagined it. Although I knew I hadn't, I knew it would be useless sharing anything else with her related to males or my feelings.

I was a junior in high school, and I had already been to seven schools, usually switching school in the middle of the school year. The day after Christmas in 1984, I was 16 years old, midway through my junior year. It was snowing, and eight below zero. My mom asked me where I was planning to go to college. I had never given it any thought, and no one at school had ever talked to me about it as I had changed schools so frequently. I had seen a basketball game on TV once, and the UCLA Bruins were playing. I liked their cute bear mascot, so I replied, "UCLA." My mom said, "Good choice—that is in California. Get Chasse (our new calico cat)—let's go."

I was dumbfounded. True, we had no money to pay rent, and the first of the month was rapidly approaching, and we were freezing cold, but to leave in an instant in our beater car during a blizzard seemed extreme even for my mom. She explained that she knew from when she lived in California that college was much more affordable than in Minnesota even at the community college level, but you had to be a resident for at least one year. I would be graduating in a year and a half, so time was of the essence.

Therefore, with Chasse shrieking in the backseat the whole way across the country, we set off with the shirts on our back and gas money in our pockets. I asked how we were going to get there, as we didn't have a map. Her response was, "Everyone knows that California is to the West. We will drive West until we hit the ocean; then we are there." That is exactly what we did. We hit terrible ice storms, and our car went off the freeway into a ditch. We walked to a coffee house until the sleet subsided. We almost died a number of times on the way, but my mom was a woman on a mission, and nothing was going to stop her. Her daughter was going to go to college.

On January 1, 1985, we arrived on the 710 Freeway that ends at the waterfront. For 14 years, I had been raised in Minnesota and was glad for it, but now I was returning to my roots, my birth state, at the age of 16. Homeless again, school-less, friendless, family-less, penniless, and with food supply uncertain, . . . I couldn't have been happier. I loved new beginnings, as I had become a master of them, writing my own script as I went. I got out of the car, shed my warm clothes, and waded out into the Pacific Ocean, knee deep. The people walking along the beachfront path looked at me as if I were crazy. To them, the natives, the water was freezing. I hollered to my mom, "Where are we?" to which she responded, "The sign says Long Beach." To which I called back, "We're home."

The party was over; now the real work began. "Go find the local high school and sign yourself up. Find a place to get a job too." I did. The registrar at the high school asked where my mom was, and I said,

"Getting a job." "Where do you live?" "We are working on that, down the block for now." The secretary looked at me in disapproval.

I walked around exploring my new city on a daily basis. My goal was to try to find a quarter on the ground every day, so I could eat. Thrifty ice cream single scoop was only 25 cents, and I found it to be filling and satisfying. I eventually also found a Taco Bell that wasn't looking for help, but I must have looked hungry and desperate, as the manager hired me to clean the giant roaches out of the urinals in the bathroom off the alley. My mom found a temporary job right away as a secretary, which led to an apartment quickly. It was official: we were Californians, and we were not going to starve, but have all the Taco Bell we could eat. Before we left, I bought a T-shirt at the mall that read, "Goodbye Minnesota, Hello California." I wanted to have one printed that read, "Goodbye McDonalds, Hello Taco Bell," but I didn't have the money. I wore my new shirt my first day of high school, and it proved to be quite a conversation starter. I made friends fast and loved every minute.

My mom was such an excellent employee that her employer soon offered her a program to get her bachelor's degree in a cohort that came out to the worksite. From there, she went on for her master's degree in vocational education. It was at this time, when my mom started to fulfill her potential, that I saw an awakening in her. She went from surviving to thriving, with a burning desire to reach back and pull up all those she could through education.

As my senior year started to wrap up, it was evident that I would be attending the local community college down the block, with the plan of transferring to a four-year university after two years. An audition came up for the musical *Hair* at the college. My mom insisted that I try out for it so I could start getting credits early and get my foot in the proverbial theatre door. I had never heard of *Hair*, although I loved musicals, and by this point had starred in many. I was a naive, virtuous 17 year old, Midwestern, Bible-toting girl whose favorite musicals were *Fiddler on the Roof*, *Godspell*, and *My Fair Lady*.

The director of *Hair* had a big name in the area for theatre productions, and it would be an honor to work with him. I remember him asking me to mess up my hair before going onstage, and I thought, *Why would I do that?* I was cast immediately, as they were looking for youthful types amongst the starring cast of veteran performers. I soon learned a completely new vocabulary that included drugs and sex, and I was mortified. I didn't want anything to do with this show. I walked home and explained what the show was about, and that I didn't feel comfortable performing in it with a cast of adult men belting out words that I didn't even know the meaning of.

She was so angered at me for saying that I didn't want to participate that she told me that if I didn't do it, and do it well, she would throw me out on the streets. She was serious. I just wanted to graduate from high school, and not be homeless, so I obeyed. My mom came to opening night and sat in the front row of the intimate theatre to witness her daughter rolling around on the floor half-naked with a dozen men singing about things she had never experienced. The look on her face said it all. She never apologized, but after that event I found my voice and started to use it, . . . and she considered it.

My mom was particularly difficult on the day of my high school graduation, criticizing my appearance and anything else she could think of. Although I had moved frequently, worked part time and attended nine schools, I graduated with honors. After the ceremony, before boarding the bus for Grad Nite at Disneyland, I asked, "Are you proud of me?" To which she replied, "I expected you to graduate from high school. There is a bachelor's' degree in you."

My friends were going to Hawaii before heading off to college. I really wanted to go, but I didn't have the money; however, I made the decision that I would one day go. My mom had gone for a time in her youth and became a Don Ho groupie. I learned this at one of the very rare times she spoke of her previous life. I came home from my job at Taco Bell to find a beautifully wrapped present on the table. I opened it, wondering what it could be. Maybe a jewelry box with a class ring in it? I untied the pink bow to reveal a typewriter. I was so relieved to have not opened it in front of her because I could not have hidden my disappointment. An electric typewriter. I could barely type. She came home, and I thanked her for the gift. She told me that I was going to need one for college, and they were expensive, so I should really take good care of it. I used it a lot, and I took great care of it.

She sat down at my new typewriter to test it. She wrote:

My three bits of wisdom for my daughter:
    1. Don't get married until after you graduate from college.
    2. Don't marry someone better looking than yourself.
    3. Don't have more children than you can afford to raise on your own.

Hmmm . . . I thought. She has learned these bits of wisdom from making these mistakes. She would get an epic fail for having failed to follow her own advice. I vowed that I would get an A plus.

I gave my mom a present that day as well. It was a thank you gift for all that she had done for me. My mom was very difficult to buy gifts for; she usually told me that she didn't like what I purchased right after opening it. This was going to be different. I was very proud of my purchase. It was a black lacquered jewelry box, with a yellow rose painted on the front, the only one in the store. It had a price tag stuck to the front of it, covering the border of the design. I purchased it none the wiser that the sticker would prove nearly impossible to remove. I eventually used nail polish remover on a piece of cotton to try to get it off. This removed the sticker and underlying glue, as well as some of the gold paint that made up the border of the rose picture. All I could notice was that quarter inch missing line of paint. I decided to buy a gold pen and repair it. No matter how hard I tried, I couldn't get my line to blend with the line already on the box. I decided to give it to my mom anyway because it was the contents inside the box that I was most excited about presenting to her.

When my mom graduated from high school, she had a job at a local discount warehouse at the jewelry counter. She bought my grandma a beautiful gold ring with an onyx stone containing a small diamond in the middle. My grandmother wore that ring every day until she died. I always thought that was such a beautiful gesture; I decided to do the same for my mom. I purchased a similar looking gold ring of black onyx stone with a diamond in the middle, and presented it to her in the jewelry box.

Although she was thankful, I am sure, the only thing she said was, "What happened to the border of the picture on the cover of the jewelry box?" That pretty much summed up how my mom saw me in all areas, always with a critical eye on my moles, never with an adoring eye on my dimple. I learned that, like my mom, roses are beautiful, but they have thorns; you have to proceed with caution when admiring them. Nonetheless, in my life I was going to focus on picking roses, not bringing attention to people's weeds as my mom had always done.

Many of my mom's decisions over her lifetime made a lasting impact on me. I tried to learn from her mistakes, of which there were plenty. Other times I noticed that I fell into the same patterns. We both married in our twenties. I feel that I was looking for male validation that I had never had since I was without a dad in my life. We both had baby girls when we were 25 and no other children. We both divorced when our daughters were two years old. We both married twice. The cycle continued. Her behaviors affected me in that I had to have constant upheaval in my life to feel "normal." I had to move frequently, and I had a general mistrust of men. I felt like I had to conquer the world, or it would conquer me. Through it all, however, God's provision and protection in my life superseded any irreparable damage that my mom could have potentially done to me. Faith continued to serve as my resiliency factor.

I continued to live with my mom. Although working full time, I went on to graduate from college in four years. On the day of my graduation ceremony, she was particularly difficult to deal with as she criticized me and the way I looked the whole drive to the event. When I met up with her after the pomp and circumstance, I asked, "Are you proud of me now?" To which she replied, "I expected you to get a bachelor's degree. There is a master's degree in you."

In spite of her harsh criticism and prickly pear personality, my mom and I remained close. We celebrated all holidays together; we would get dressed up and go to Downtown Disney. Mickey and Minnie were a regular part of our holiday photos; Easter, Mother's Day, Thanksgiving, and Christmas were all spent in the shadow of the Mouse House.

My mom continued her education, earning her master's degree in vocational education leadership. She became adjunct faculty at numerous local community colleges, teaching paralegal skills and computer applications in addition to her full-time job during the days. My mom gave her time, talent, and treasure toward helping others where she was employed. She changed lives of inner city African American students in Los Angeles, as she put together summer camps and educational programs so the students could enjoy these opportunities free of charge.

She gave money out of her own pocket to the international students who were employed at the camps she organized to make sure they had a great time visiting tourist destinations like Disneyland and Universal Studios while in California. She traveled alone from high school to high school in the toughest parts of Los Angeles, teaching students how to write resumes, interview, and get a career.

She was a leader in the Cambodian community, where she assisted in developing education programs and got grants to fund computer labs for the youth. She was a leader in the Samoan community, where she taught vocational classes and empowered the students to move ahead in their careers and lives. She ran a program that specialized in helping homeless and troubled Latino students get a fresh start in life, along with an education and career.

One of my favorite Thanksgiving memories was when she paid for all of the students who had nowhere to go for Thanksgiving to have a meal at the local Hometown Buffet. She asked me to join her since I had nowhere to go either. One by one, the students went around the table and said what they were thankful for. It was a large room full of students, and every one spoke of how my mom had changed their lives in so many ways, adding that there was no other family that they would rather be with on Thanksgiving. There was not a dry eye in the building.

My mom was fearless. We were driving home from a work event she hosted late one night, and we were lost in a particularly rough part of Los Angeles. We couldn't afford a Thomas Guide. I saw two men involved in a drug deal a little way down in a deserted area in an alley. I told her that we needed to leave the area, and she said, "What we need is directions." She proceeded to get out of the car despite my protesting and marched up to the men, who looked shocked to see this older white woman approaching them confidently and asking for directions. They shoved the baggies in their pockets and gave her detailed directions. She got back in the car and said, "What nice young men; let's go home." And we did.

Every year in the spring at graduation time, she bought each one of the students she was working with a graduation gift. Some years it was a silver photo frame, other years a leather pad portfolio, calculators, pens—whatever she could afford. She felt strongly that every student deserved a graduation acknowledgment gift, as most would receive none from others.

My mom barely made any money at these nonprofit agencies, and she would pour every dime of hers back into the students she served. Even if that meant that she went without eating for a period of time or being able to pay her rent. She even went as far as living in an abandoned mini silver jet Airstream travel trailer in a rough neighborhood in order to supply more for the students she served. Changing the lives of the disenfranchised and marginalized populations in Southern California became her life's passion.

She continued to serve at church as well. She was a Sunday school teacher for thirty years, and she rarely missed a day. Even in my youth, when we had nothing, I had many Laotian, Cambodian, and Thai friends who were recent refugees. She bought them clothes and took them with us wherever we went. She modeled for me loving those in need and giving generously.

I remember one time in my youth when she worked as a secretary at a wealthy law office. Typically, they would send a check from the business annually to a local nonprofit that focused on helping young African American males in Minneapolis. My mom called the nonprofit center to offer the check and asked if they needed anything else. The nonprofit requested a big picnic for the boys with the employees of the law firm.

She organized the biggest full-day picnic event I had ever seen. Children arrived literally by the busload. At first, the lawyers appeared overwhelmed. They drove their expensive cars behind the buses that picked up the children in the roughest parts of town. I could see the look of disappointment on my mom's face. She said, "Get on the bus; we ride with the children, not in our own car. We will come back and get it later. You are going to lead a large group today and make sure your team wins so they leave proud and with big prizes." I was 12 years old; some of the boys were my age. My team won; they left with many prizes, and more importantly, with pride.

The lawyers boarded the bus on the way home and left their cars behind to retrieve later. When we got home exhausted, my mom turned to me and said, "There will always be someone prettier than you, smarter than you, and richer than you, but no matter how little you have, you give all that you have got." She added, "I am impressed by how you led today." I had worked 12 years for this moment, to hear my mom say she was pleased with me; I worked daily for the next thirty years to get to hear it again. Compliments were extremely rare from my mom, almost nonexistent. I felt like I had won the biggest prize I could ever obtain. My mom had complimented me!

Later in life, working full time as a teacher, leading church ministries part time, and being a single mom to a three-year-old daughter, I forged ahead to earn a master's degree. Here again, my mom was her typical graduation day self, harping on me about every little thing that I did; of course, I could do no right, everything was wrong, including even how I hold my mouth when at rest. She thought I looked like I was frowning. I met up with her after the ceremony and said, "Mom, are you proud of me?" to which she replied, "I expected you to get a master's degree. You have a doctorate in you."

As time and the years went on, our degrees were affording us opportunities to shop, dine, and travel, as we were never able to before. Finally, our hard work was paying off, and we rewarded ourselves with vacations. By this time, I was a divorced single mom with a daughter myself, so we became the three musketeers traveling to Disney World, Mexico, France, England, Minnesota, The Bahamas, . . . and the list goes on.

When my mom was 52, she moved in with me for a period, as, here again, she had given all she had and had no savings or credit opportunities. She woke up one day and told me that there were homeless people living in the house that we rented. She was adamant that the government was watching her through the cable lines, etc. I was 27 and suddenly a single mom with serious personal issues of my own going on, so I chose to ignore this. She was a high-functioning person who was loved by students and coworkers by day but was impossible to live with because of what I referred to her as her craziness by night. My daughter and I soon moved out of our own place to get some physical distance.

She continued to live on her own and work. She always lived nearby. We spoke on the phone daily. We shopped and had lunch every weekend at the minimum. We would run into my friends in the community, and one even commented that it looked like I was in a bad situation with my mom being so verbally abusive toward me. As much as I was embarrassed, I was partly edified that others saw what I felt and that it wasn't just my perception of the situation. It felt like she was taking out years of pain on me.

At age 65, my mom, who vowed she would never retire, retired from her full-time day job very suddenly in December of 2008. I showed up at her work unannounced; I had never met her coworkers, and I was trying to make sense of the sudden change of heart. She was well loved by the judges and her colleagues; they acted equally surprised at the turn of events. I bought her a dozen yellow roses to congratulate her and used it as a guise to visit her.

She had a horrible episode (what she referred to as a sunburn, but to me looked more like shingles) that lasted for months. Again she refused to go to the doctor; her students even begged her to get medical attention. It was painful to look at. She continued to teach at the local community college in the evenings.

She began telling me stories of how some of her students were terrorists who were contacting their organizations during class time on the college computers—she was fearful. I figured it was some kind of misunderstanding; as she was so together in all other aspects of her life, I ignored the mention of it. I told her that if she really felt someone were dangerous she should contact the school administration, which apparently she did.

I didn't realize what was happening until the dean at the community college where she worked called me as her emergency contact to inform me that my mom was having some "mental issues." He didn't want to expound on what had happened, but he wanted me to be aware so I could get her help. She had been one of their all-time favorite professors. It was the end of the term, and I asked him to consider her as retired; he agreed to label the situation as such. I am sure this was a difficult call for him to make, and I am so thankful that he did. I let my mom know what had happened, and she surprisingly agreed, although she felt that I was conspiring with whomever was making her life a living hell.

I had no idea that on June 16, 2009, my mom had experienced a psychotic break. It wasn't until July 7 that she left a mysterious voicemail for me, accusing me of paying people to rape her. I had better stop, or she was going to contact the authorities.

I was in such a state of shock that I took my dogs and got in the car headed to the beach to sit, pray, and try to sort everything out mentally before responding to her accusations. It was Tuesday; I had just had lunch with her the previous Sunday. I had spoken with her on the phone the night before, and all had seemed well.

While stopping for a light, I looked back to check on my dogs in the backseat and gently rear-ended the car in front of me. It was a minor fender bender. The driver told me that although there was no visible damage to his car, and no air bags or anything had gone off, he was going to try to get free massages out of the insurance company, which he did. I called for a tow as my front bumper had some damage, and the tow truck driver got into a fistfight with a man who hit my car while being loaded up on the tow truck. The police had to come. In the meantime, I contacted Jean to pick up my dogs and me, although she was in the final stages of cancer. Little did I know that she would die about 14 weeks later. On top of my current issues, I had a litany of other personal issues going on that were paramount in my mind. I learned a lesson that day to never drive while preoccupied.

I went home to be met with a letter under my door from my mom. It was addressed to me, the police department, and over 200 universities, public officials, and research programs. This included the president of the United States. After her death, I found on her computer that she had actually emailed it to everyone listed.

To Whom It May Concern:

In the event of my death this evening, I would like to communicate the following facts that have transpired over the past weeks. I have been the subject of a hospice agency or research encompassing holistic health and surveillances related to virtual reality ranging from programs in the Circle of Life/Love Matchmaking and blood transfusions and bloodletting to hate/hurt motive testing of drugs similar to that done in Sweden involving microwave technology, as well as brain computer imagery and biomedical and synthetic telepathy to implant teeth.

Hence, my writing to you to determine if I am on a subject list for one or more of your clinical research trials, and if so, please take me off. I need this madness stopped. Every part of it is criminal, from beginning to end. It has ruined my retirement. At my age, there are not that many more years left and each one becomes more valuable.

I do have hard evidence to support my claims, including a laser rod with three colored pouches, a blood clot with three ¼-inch molar teeth, and a large portion of fat removed from my person to accommodate their work—all of which have come through my body and I have been able to capture.

(I discovered all of these specimens when cleaning out her apartment after her death. The autopsy concluded that she had extensive uterine cancer and teeth that had rotted out of her mouth that she had ingested.)

I also kept a daily dairy.

(She did this for 19 months prior to her death.)

According to the written reports, the program is designed to send you to a sanatorium, to drive you mad as you constantly are hearing voices. I told the perpetrators from the beginning, and throughout that, I did not want to be a part of whatever it was.

Later, as I tried to record some of it, I was told that I was the only one who could hear the music, speaker, pounding, etc.

(I later found numerous audio and video tapes where she attempted to record what was happening to her.)

Soon after a whole military battle reenactment played out virtually, complete with gun battle, in my living room. It was as if they were in my apartment performing a scene that belonged on a stage.

With constant loud, annoying music and voices blaring from the walls of my apartment throughout the evening and day hours, I was forced to live in fear of a crazed Tom Dooley, the singer and keyboard artist for the first event. He put on an act that he was in love with me, and every time they came to pick him up in the late evening, he would refuse to go. He sang love songs to me, asking me to marry him, promising me the world, then hiding out in the rafters (which were probably virtual as well), he frightened me throughout the day and evening, to the point that I would stand up for as much as 6 hours waiting for his handlers to remove him so I could bathe. You see, he had access to viewing everything I did, everything I thought, and to the extent that even in my car and at work he was present singing tunes over and over again at the top of his lungs. He came in and raped me, and held me captive for over a week. . . . I haven't slept one night since June 15. You establish a relationship which is strong affection (you can't help yourself) and that you must keep control of the situation. At 1:16 this morning, I was to climb the mountain with him (they use heat to do that so you wake up as a non-participant but with a feeling of floating).

My daughter will think that I am crazy, that walls do not talk. The singer said that my daughter set the whole thing up. She signed the contract, and she is liable for paying the balance. She owes $150,000 dollars. When I go places with my daughter, they go with us. As far as my daughter ordering this, she would have had to have Power of Attorney from me authorizing her to sign, and I certainly haven't given her one. I think she is sexually abusing others.

Please look into this matter, and respond if you know something about it.

Sincerely,

MD

PS The Department of the Navy has a teddy bear robot that they are testing as well.

I stood in shock, in total disbelief. I knew it was all in her head, especially the part about my involvement in this torture and her allegations against me. I was terrified and intrigued at the same time. I needed more information, so I decided to pay her a visit the next day.

I slept with the chair in front of my front door and two dogs at my sides, as she had the keys to my house. When I got up, I went to her apartment to ask if we could talk about the letter; she acted as if it were no big deal and wanted to go to lunch and shopping. She refused to discuss it. I told her I was there to listen for the voices to find out if I could hear anything, and that I was concerned for her and trying to understand and support her.

She thought I was ridiculous sitting in silence listening and looking around. I told her I could lose my job and daughter based on her allegations, and she just ignored me, but I could see that something in her eyes was different; she didn't look the same. She had the look of a person who was not herself, and she didn't know who she was. I did the hardest thing imaginable for me: I asked her for my keys back. I made up some lame excuse about losing my spare set, and she relented. It pained me to not be able to trust the only person I had in the world left that I was close to. There were periods of life where she had been my only and best friend, and now I feared my mom—and my mom, me.

I spent the next 19 months trying to solve this mystery as I dealt with the death of my best friend amongst other issues that were vying for my undivided attention. I was at a loss. Just prior to my best friend's death, she recommended a book about paranoid schizophrenia. Its contents changed my life. I then knew what I was dealing with. How could I, as a professor of School Counseling and Psychology, not have understood what was going on with my own mom? Perhaps it was my own defense mechanism, as I wasn't ready to handle it at the time.

I contacted my dad, which was no easy task. I had to leave a message with the bookstore in town and ask them to let him use the phone to call me if they ever saw him. I even begged him to be in a right mind so I could ask him questions about my mom and whether she had heard voices in her twenties when he knew her. He did pull himself together mentally for the first time in years, and we had our first "sane" conversation I could recall. He denied knowing anything. Others who had known her all responded in kind, saying that she was a private person, so they had no idea.

I contacted her landlord, who was a retired psychiatrist, and we met with my mom to no avail. She "played normal" so well. She took excellent care of herself. She never drank or used drugs. There was no outward sign of anything going on with her, not even visible in her apartment. I called the local police department to see if they would hospitalize her; they stood next to me, unbeknownst to her, as I talked with her at the door. She denied wanting to hurt herself or others, and that anyone was hurting her, so their hands were tied.

I called my friends who were psychologists for advice. Nothing. My mom had no friends or relatives to lean on or who could offer assistance. She had no attachments to neighbors or anyone in the community. The only time I was met with great opposition with her was when I asked her to go to the doctor, to which she responded angrily that she knew I was the one who was having her tortured. She was physically stronger than I, perhaps in part from all those years of shoveling snow, and there was no way I could physically control her in any way, shape, or form. I prayed continually for wisdom and strength.

Although she would appear well dressed, and frequently looked beautiful in all white, our lunch and shopping dates became fewer and further between. She didn't join me at Downtown Disney at her favorite restaurant for holidays or my birthday. She would always make up an excuse. We continued to talk on the phone, but she would spend the whole conversation pushing numbers on the phone, as she thought she was being directed by the voices to enter information about her health. Even though she had no musical training at all, she spoke of a musical she was writing, and a book she was self-publishing regarding education. This was based in reality and clearly was her therapy. The book incidentally was ahead of its time and contained a brilliant analysis of education reform that is very popular today.

On February 2, 2010, on what would have been my best friend's birthday, on my insistence I took her to dinner to celebrate her book being published. She wasn't herself at all. She would barely open her mouth; I didn't realize she had lost teeth. She thought that they had been removed from her as an experiment in pain. She dedicated her book to God, stating, "To the Lord, who keeps me going each day." It was unusual for my mom to make a public proclamation of faith, especially in her later years. She started attending church again as well. Additionally, she hand-wrote a dedication in my copy of the book, "To my daughter, Bobbi—your love sustains me through all things. May the strength of your convictions, the power of your faith, and the sharing of your love make a difference in all that you do. Love, Mom, 02/02/10." What peace to recognize that she knew I loved her.

We continued to white knuckle it through life. The last time I saw her was Martin Luther King Jr. Day, 2011. I was passing by her house and asked her to come out and say hi to me, and to the dogs. She wore all white; her eyes still had that empty glaze to them. We exchanged niceties, and she petted the dogs through the car window. A still, small voice said inside me, "It won't be long now." I had to make an excuse to pull away as I was so caught off guard.

It wasn't as though I were hearing external voices like my mom, but as though my Holy Spirit internally had shared knowledge with me. I had no reason to believe my mom was physically ill. She was a strong woman who could live to 100 with her mental illness. Was she suicidal? Homicidal? I kept in constant contact with the landlord who lived next to her and kept a watchful eye on her. I frequently made excuses to come by, and spent many hours driving all over the city looking for her after she would disappear, since she was angry at me for supporting the ongoing torture.

February 1, 2011, I hadn't heard from her, and I had been leaving multiple voice messages. I decided to go looking for her. Her car was not in its port at her apartment. I eventually found her walking out of the grocery store with a dozen yellow roses in her hand, smiling from ear to ear. She had never bought herself flowers before. She got into her car and started talking to herself, but she looked happy.

She carried her flowers, groceries, and Subway sandwich up to her apartment, and I drove away with her none the wiser that I had followed her. When I got home I called my mom; even though it was late, I felt compelled to check on her. She answered in a voice that sounded like she was hurting. I asked her what was wrong, and she said she had a stomachache. I offered to take some Pepto to her, and she adamantly declined; she said it wasn't that kind of pain. I asked her if she wanted me to come over or get help, and she flatly declined again. She started hitting the numbers on her phone in accordance with the directions that the voices were giving her. She sounded tired. She said she was going to bed. I told her I would call her tomorrow.

I worked February 2, 2011, from 7:30 a.m. to 10:00 p.m. I was to organize my best friend's birthday memorial at her favorite restaurant that night, but I couldn't get off work as a professor at a local university; they didn't have any substitutes. It was the beginning of the term, and I was a new employee. Class went until late, and I dutifully called my mom, feeling in my Holy Spirit that something was not right. Perhaps it was because I was missing my best friend. I had a voice message from my mom when I got home. She sounded different, tired, and weak. She said only, "Take care of yourself. I love you, and I am proud of you." I had waited 42 years to hear those words. I knew in my heart that it was finished.

I called her, and the phone rang and rang. I prayed that she would answer, and I prayed that she would not.

Just as when I was a little girl I had been paralyzed in fear and didn't show up in time to save my mom from my dad's blow. Just as when I was a teenager, I had been paralyzed in fear and didn't show up and take action to save my mom from her attacker. Now I was a grown woman, I was paralyzed in fear, and I didn't show up in time to save my mom from her impending death.

Instead, I prayed for no regrets; I told God that I was afraid that she had committed suicide, or had lost her mind and lay in wait to kill me. It was late, and I was alone. I had a full list of reasons and excuses to not run over to her rescue. I called her house again and left her a message that I loved her, and I would come to her house soon if I didn't hear from her. I moved the chair in front of the door and went to bed.

I awoke with a start first thing the next morning. I got dressed and proceeded to her house. Her little blue Chevy was in its spot. I pounded on her door. I told her loudly (hoping the neighbors would hear) that I was coming in with my copy of the key. I cracked the door open ever so slightly and called her name repeatedly. I moved my eyes around the apartment from the front door. I looked down and saw her foot next to the door; she had collapsed in front of the door. At that moment, the smell of death overwhelmed me. I retreated and closed the door as I gasped for fresh air while I was trying to hold back tears and figure out what to do. I called 911. I stood at the top of the steps outside. I didn't want to see her like this, and I certainly didn't want them to think I had anything to do with her death. The tears overwhelmed me, and I grasped the cold iron handle rail of the stairs, doubled over in emotion. Part pain, part relief, part hysterical, part in peace.

The coroner was a beautiful young woman who looked like she had just stepped out of an episode of *CSI* in her black trench coat. She looked more like a supermodel than someone who dabbled in death all day. I was so in shock I remember asking her if she liked her job, to which she replied, "I used to find it fascinating until I had children of my own. I get called out on a lot of children's cases, and I am finding that I like it less." She explained to me that my mom had died the night before. I still can't figure out why the paramedics asked me if she had a Do Not Resuscitate order. There was no hope for that at the point I found her. I know CPR, but from the stench there was clearly no need. Even the paramedic had to cover his mouth and back away. He looked over to me to see if I noticed. I had, but I understood.

They removed her body and opened the windows to air the place out. The coroner would contact me with the results of the autopsy. I went back to the apartment the next day. My mom would never share any private information with me, like her social security number or anything related to her finances, etc. She would never discuss end-of-life matters with me, or her wishes. She once said in anger after my best friend had died that she wanted to be cremated with no memorial service. She and Jean had always shared a special bond, and now they would share a date of remembrance as well. I thought this was somehow poetic.

I searched the apartment for clues. She had made out her rent check but didn't deliver it on time, which was unlike her. I dropped it off, which bought me the month to clean everything out. I covered the bloodstain on the carpet with an area rug.

I sat and stared at the yellow roses on her table that she had recently bought herself. They too were poetic, my mom and her life were like roses—thorny, yet beautiful.

I discovered on her desk a pile of papers. They were typewritten and dated. She chronicled a comprehensive journal of the last 19 months of torture that she had suffered. She had no idea that she had advanced stage uterine cancer, nor that she suffered from late onset paranoid schizophrenia; neither did I at the time. I flipped through the hundreds of pages of detailed description of her demise. August 14, 2010: "... I don't fear for my life, as I have faith, and that faith has seen me through thus far ..."

Her last entry was on January 23, 2011, about a week prior to her death. She wrote that she had been diligent and thorough in her writings, as she was doing it for science, to help future law students fight for freedom from elder abuse and technological health laws and human research without consent. That was my mom, the quintessential educator until the very end.

Although she owned very little, and certainly nothing of any financial value, she had secret hoarding tendencies. Piles of shoes, a cupboard filled with half used Bath and Body Works products, and pile upon pile of paper containing unopened mail and former student work.

Fortunately for me, she lived in a small senior apartment. The elderly woman who lived downstairs came over and said she had heard a loud boom the night before and thought that perhaps my mom had taken a fall. My mom was the youngest, by far, of those who resided in the complex, and the woman assumed that she was okay.

This made me wonder if my mother had ever heard my voice message; I decided in my mind that she had. Was she waiting for me to come over and rescue her at the last moment? Was she at the door because she was unlocking it so I could gain easy access? I told myself that neither had been the case. I continued to clean, and I donated almost everything.

As I approached the donation box at the front door, I felt a sudden sharp pain grip my chest. I had never experienced anything like it in my life. I couldn't breathe. I was sure that I was dying of a massive heart attack, that my body just couldn't take any more stress. I grabbed my chest and prayed to myself, "God, help me." I looked down and saw the area rug below me covering the stains that were physical evidence of my mom's death in that exact place where I stood. I said to myself, "Please, Jesus—not here, not now." The pain completely retreated in an instant. I felt great. It was as if it had never happened. I had renewed energy and vigor. I didn't even need to sit down.

I continued to run up and down the stairs throwing away piles of junk mail. Suddenly, my Holy Spirit told me to go to the trash and re-cover a mailer from AARP (American Association of Retired Persons). I couldn't believe that I was digging through trash for unopened junk mail for no real reason. Once it was located, I saw that the front of the envelope said something about AARP members being eligible to purchase life insurance.

My mom had no savings and only the amount of her rent in checking. She had never mentioned life insurance or anything like it. I felt compelled to call to see whether she had a policy already in existence, although I doubted it. She did! I was able to pay off her bills and get her cremated! She had no will and did not list me as a beneficiary on anything, but with this money I was able to fulfill my dream of returning to Minnesota to walk down memory lane in her honor.

I needed to get away. The blue super shuttle picked me up before dawn. I was on my way to LAX, north of my home. The driver took us south toward Orange County, which I thought was odd, but I didn't think much of it. I figured we had other passengers to pick up before proceeding to the airport. I was exhausted and sleepy from getting up so early. The driver spoke minimal English, so we didn't really talk much. He had no idea where I was going, or why.

All of a sudden I looked up, and he was parked outside of my mom's former apartment. It is located in an awkward area in the back of a complex where there are only a handful of spots off the main road. He pulled the shuttle into her former parking spot. We sat in silence. I thought, "How odd that we are picking someone up who lived in my mom's former, yet recent, apartment building." No one came out, the driver didn't move.

I started to get a little creeped out by the whole experience, and I asked him, "What are we doing just sitting here?" He replied, "I don't know." I was shocked into silence. Am I going to become a victim? Are people going to read about me in the morning newspapers? I wasn't into ghosts, but was my mom's spirit going to come out and haunt me?

I started to pray in panic. It was dark, and there was no one around. I was locked in the back seat; I didn't know what to do. After what seemed to be forever, he said, "I must be lost." Then he started the shuttle and drove me to the airport. In my heart, I felt like we had picked up my mom to return to Minnesota with me. We loved to travel, and from then on I had peace about her death and my role in it. I knew in my heart that she had known that I had never done her any intentional harm, that I only showed her love and respect even in those times I never received any in return.

In Minnesota, I visited my maternal grandparents' gravesite. I took yellow roses. I walked around my former neighborhoods where I had resided with my mom. I saw the house where she had accidentally slammed my hand in the car door. I went to my stepdad's house and spent time outside my grandma's as well. I found peace in the journey.

When I arrived home, I created a memorial card and mailed it to about fifty people who had known my mom through past jobs, as well as other acquaintances. They kindly offered their condolences, and the sympathy cards came pouring in. One card read, "She was an inspiration and role model for women, especially single mothers, as she pursued her dreams, and achieved so many accomplishments."

I even sent a memorial card to the president because my mom would have wanted me to. She loved politics. I spread her ashes on President's Day in Long Beach near the place where we had pulled into town in January of 1985. It was a quiet, still morning, but when I placed her ashes in the water it stirred vigorously. I looked around to see if there were any boats or wind around me, and there were none. The air was eerily still. I threw yellow rose petals in the water and said a prayer. One of the petals followed me all the way back to the car, bounding along the sidewalk.

I spent the year following her death processing what had transpired. Her official post mortem diagnosis came in as uterine cancer with clinical schizophrenia based on the evidence I had provided. I learned that schizophrenia is when you interpret reality abnormally, hallucinate, and have delusions and disordered thinking. It is rarely diagnosed after age 45. Late onset cases only affect .1–.4 percent of the population.

I also applied for a doctoral program at the local university. I took the entrance test the week after she died. I was still in a state of shock. I got to the math portion and, once again, just entered "c" for every answer. Turns out I scored better on math than I had ever done in my life. I used my mom's book on educational reform as an inspiration to write my dissertation on the same topic. I graduated three years later. My name was called over the loudspeaker; I looked up into the sky. I imagined my best friend, Jean, cheering me on at her alma mater. I could picture her saying, "High five from Jean!" Next to her, I pictured my mom with a big smile on her face. I said to myself, "Mom, are you proud of me?" And I heard her responding, "Bobbi, I love you, and I am proud of you, but I know you have a book in you." I grinned and accepted my diploma as I exited the stage in victory.

On December 6, 2011, about ten months after her death, in honor of what would have been her birthday, I had a memorial brick installed at a Navy statue that overlooks the Pacific Ocean, close to where we first arrived in town, and near her final workplace. I sat on the bench, looked at the vast ocean before me, and reflected on my mom and the legacy she left to me. She had so many strengths; she was gifted in writing, and she enjoyed baseball: the Twins, Dodgers, and Angels. She would sit and watch school board meetings on TV for hours as her two great loves, education and politics, kissed. She enjoyed shoe shopping and going out to eat. Although used sparingly, she had an infectious laugh and a smile that could light up a room.

More than that, she taught me life lessons that I am so grateful for: she taught me a strong work ethic, perseverance, to seize adventure; she taught me to be strong, independent, and to value education. To have faith. She exemplified self-sacrificial love throughout her lifetime. The value of helping others, especially the disenfranchised and marginalized, succeed through education. Not only did she give me physical life, but she taught me *how* to live; more importantly, she introduced me to eternal life by taking me to church every Sunday. I was allowed to grow and believe as I chose, but she planted that seed that eventually made me bloom into the Christian woman I am today. What more could I ever ask or hope for?

I placed a yellow rose on her brick and headed to the car. Christmas was coming, my favorite time of year. One of my favorite aspects is the music. My mom was a major Elvis fan. We were groupies for a local impersonator who I think she liked even more than Elvis himself. The Christmas right before she died, I got her a CD of Elvis Christmas music. I found it while cleaning out her apartment, unopened. I tore off the plastic wrapper and put it in the CD player. As I pulled into my driveway at home, the last song came on, and it had nothing to do with Christmas. Elvis crooned, "Momma loved roses, I left them on her grave." Tears welled up in my eyes, and spilled all over my cheeks. I knew it was going to be another long winter, but this time I knew there would be roses.

I could never list all of the important life lessons I learned from my mom, but I have listed some of the highlights:

Life lessons from my mom (Maybeth): she taught me:
1. Embrace a strong work ethic.
2. Persevere, and be strong in the face of adversity.
3. Seize adventure.
4. Be independent (take care of yourself).
5. Value education.
6. Have faith.
7. Help others, especially the disenfranchised and marginalized, succeed through education.
8. Go to a church.
9. Don't have more children than you can raise well on your own.
10. Perhaps most importantly, let a cake cool prior to adding icing.

4.
Jack's Box

This fourth box contains items that belonged to my dad. In it are old books, pictures, and a collection of writings. My dad was quite a character, and I loathed seeing him. At my parents' divorce hearing when I was two, the judge still felt it appropriate for him to have unsupervised visits with me on the weekends because he had never hit me. It was the early 1970s, and divorce was not as common in our area, and even though the courts still favored mothers, dads retained many rights. I considered writing the judge in my teens to let him know he had made the wrong decision to make me see my dad, but I figured no one is perfect, and he was just trying to give my dad another chance. Overall, the judge probably had my best interest in mind even though he had a lack of understanding regarding domestic violence and how it can affect a child. My mom was of no use to put a stop to the visits, as she feared my dad for good reason, and she had no money for a lawyer. She had also been very close to her dad; I could tell that she secretly hoped my dad would pull his life together so I could have a relationship with him, as she did with her dad. I am so thankful that God protected me in spite of the judge's ruling and my mom's inability to take action. While God became my Father, my dad became a stranger whom I feared.

I am looking at a photo of my dad and me sitting in the front yard. It was the last photo taken of us together before he left for California. I remember that when I was very young he arrived at our doorstep to pick me up on a Saturday morning, drunk as usual, and running hours late. My mom said he couldn't take me away from home; he could visit me in the yard. I was worried that a physical altercation would ensue, as that was his nature, but he surprisingly complied. He took me out front, where the cars and busses were buzzing by. We lived at the corner of a busy intersection. There was a large tree stump in our front yard. We sat on the grass next to the stump. My dad prided himself on knowing *all* things, especially pertaining to nature. He told me to count the rings on the stump, as they represented years of the tree's life prior to its being cut down and killed. I wasn't even school age, and I struggled to count all the rings; he had to help me. He explained what the tree would be used for after it was cut down.

I asked, "What do you think happens to people after they die?"

"They go into the wild blue yonder."

"Do you mean heaven?"

"No, the wild blue yonder."

"That's not what my Sunday school teacher said. She said if we believe in Jesus, we go to heaven."

"Listen to your dad; you hear me, pal?"

"You betcha, pal."

"Swell, pal, I gotta go."

At that, he gave me a quick bear hug and a big slobbery kiss on my lips that I hated, and he ran for the bus pulling up to the corner, leaving me alone in the front yard. I walked back into the house. My mom inquired about what we talked about. I replied, "Dad is going to hell."

As an adult, I never was able to figure out why my dad lacked a moral compass. Although I never met him, I know that my paternal grandfather was the black sheep of an otherwise robust Mormon heritage. I am so thankful to them for retaining such accurate family records and spiritual memoirs to get a sense of who they are and what they believe. My ancestors were not only practicing Mormons, but were a part of the original 18 or so who founded the religion in the Idaho and Utah region. I heard that my great-grandfather died printing the book of Mormon, literally, from the ink used at that time.

My grandfather left for the California redwoods, where he owned property adjacent to the Avenue of the Giants, and spent his days drinking and chopping down the redwoods to sell. He felt he looked like actor John Barrymore. He would always turn profile in pictures, as he wanted to show off his Barrymore nose. He was tall and thin.

My paternal grandmother was his first wife. They divorced soon after my dad, their only child, was born, due to my grandpa's drinking. It is rumored that my grandfather killed his second wife in a boating "accident." He never remarried again. The only thing in this box of my grandfather's are letters written to my dad just prior to my birth, begging him to stop drinking. He admits that he destroyed his life and the lives of others due to his alcoholism and begs his son to not make the same mistake.

My paternal grandmother was raised in Washington. Her family was devout in their Norwegian Lutheran faith. They donated the land to the church, and my great-grandfather served as the architect for the building. My grandma and her siblings spent a lot of time in those church walls growing up. My grandma had red hair that would have made Lucille Ball jealous. Although her name was Emma, everyone called her Rusty due to her beautiful hair. She was tall and thin. She loved to dress up and had a penchant for scarves. She spent much of her childhood in a sanitarium due to contracting TB, and her family was rarely able to visit her. She was sickly a lot as a child. Just when she was getting stronger, a person threw a pot of flaming wax out the window of a house, and it was strewn all over the back of Rusty's bare legs. She sustained serious burns that put her on crutches until a friend took her to her church, where they had a healing service, and she walked out crutch free, never to use them again, her walking completely normal. She went on to be a waitress in Oakland, where she met her third husband, the love of her life. She was so skilled a waitress that she maintained a perfect cash register for two years in a row—not one error. She set a local record. In her later years, she sent sympathy, congratulatory, and get well cards to every stranger she saw printed in the paper. This was her ministry.

With such a strong faith-based genealogy, one would think that my dad may have inherited some of that sense of serving a higher calling or purpose in life, yet he lacked all direction and purpose. He even went as far as to get an attorney to try to get the land back from the church that his family had donated and raised from the ground up, for his *own* benefit!

My grandmother raised my dad in Oakland, and he visited his dad frequently in Myers Flat, a small town with under 200 in population in Northern California. By age 13, he was couch surfing, running away, and staying at the YMCA, although he wrote that he had a loving mother and loved his stepdad as if he were his own dad. He even referred to him as Dad and took on his last name at school. He had started drinking to the point of being drunk on a daily basis, and he never stopped until the day he died. He also really cared for his stepmother.

He was estranged from both of his parents. His parents died within two weeks of each other. Both had long-term illness, and he knew that they were close to death. Although he was local, he didn't visit either and didn't attend their funerals or visit their gravesites for years. Their only child too drunk to show up and pay his final respects.

Really, I feel that my dad stole my relationship with my grandparents from me, as he had no relationship with them, and they didn't really want him to know where they were, so they stopped reaching out to me. My mom made numerous attempts over the years, even taking me to visit in California and having my grandma out for a visit in Minnesota, but the distance was too great, and contact dwindled over time. This was just another residual aspect of the fallout that my dad created by making choices that destroyed numerous lives. He even robbed me of my grief.

One time when I was almost five years old, my mom and I went to visit my grandma in California; we took an overnight Greyhound bus trip between Seattle and Los Gatos. It was June, and it was Northern California; the bus was packed with many migrant workers. United States Immigration officers stopped our bus en route at about 3:00 a.m. in the middle of nowhere. The officers came on board the bus and made the announcement to all the passengers that everyone needed to show their green cards or be removed from the bus.

I was terrified; I didn't know what a green card was. I had a small deck of souvenir playing cards my mom had purchased for me on the trip. I quickly rifled through them, looking for a green one, to no avail. I was panicked. I didn't know how I was going to produce one of those cards in the middle of the night on that lonely highway. The officer looked at my mom and me and moved on to the next people. No questions asked; we didn't have to show a green card for some reason. All of the other passengers on that bus were removed. The driver continued down the road with only us left as passengers. I asked my mom where all the people were going to go. She replied, "I don't know. Pray for them."

Even though over the years my dad left his parents alone, he visited me sometimes when I was a very small child. My mom told a story about when he babysat me while she ran to the store. He put me on the bed and went in the other room to get drunk. When she returned soon after, I was missing. I had fallen into the crack between the bed and the wall. My dad was passed out drunk on the bed. Our dog, Benji, sniffed me out and alerted her to my whereabouts. My mom thought I had been kidnapped. Not long after, my dad let Benji out of the front door even though my mom warned him not to. He ran into the street and was struck by a car and died. That was the official end of the relationship. She had endured his alcoholism and domestic violence, but killing the dog was the deal breaker. From that day on, she secretly looked for a way out.

Visits from my dad were always fraught with fear. He would stumble up the front steps for his Saturday visit.

"Jack, you are drunk!"

"No, I'm not; give me my daughter!"

The drama would go on and on, and out of my mom's fear, my dad usually won.

"Where are you taking her?"

"To the library in downtown Minneapolis."

"It's freezing outside, Jack."

"We will take the city bus."

"Bobbi, do you remember our phone number?" I nodded. I knew the drill. Find a police officer or a woman with children, tell them my name, and ask them to call my mom. I was not even school aged, and I knew all of my personal information by heart. She always put a coin in my pocket and told me to give it to someone to call her since I couldn't reach it myself. We got about a block away from the house, and my dad instructed me to stick out my thumb in a hitchhiker pose. He didn't have money for a bus, as usual. Right away, a man pulled over. We got in with me alone in the back seat. The man said to my dad, "What are you doing? It is freezing outside, and hitchhiking is very dangerous. I only pulled over to protect the child." My dad and the man got into a fight, and we were dropped off. He told me to not tell my mom, and off we went.

"Are we going to the library?"

"No, we are going to a . . . restaurant."

"We are? You didn't have money for the bus."

We walked into the restaurant. He told me to sit on a stool in the corner. He ordered beer. After he had a few drinks, the waitress came over to me and asked if I had a mom because she felt that my mom needed to know where I was. I gave her my coin and my phone number. She returned my dime and called my mom, and the waitress continued to serve my dad. My mom showed up quickly and took me with her, thanking the waitress profusely. When my mom was paid, she had me wait in the car back at the "restaurant" and told me she wanted to thank the woman who had helped me. That server was our hero!

I wasn't always that lucky, however. One day he took me to an "all you can eat" cafeteria in Minneapolis. He told me I could take whatever

I wanted, so I loaded up my tray. He told me to eat while we were still in line collecting the food. I wanted to sit down, but he told me we were in a hurry. We got up to the cash register, and they had balloons for kids. He took a balloon for me, and I was so excited. The cashier told him the amount, and he said that he didn't have any money. She said she was calling the police.

He grabbed my hand and whisked me toward the door with my red balloon on a stick bobbing in the breeze. I felt terrible that we had stolen; I was afraid of being arrested and making Jesus sad. I wriggled away when we were down the block. I ran as fast as my little legs would carry me back to the restaurant. I ran to the cashier, and there was now a manager with her. I yelled, "I am sorry I ate food that I didn't pay for. I will wash the dishes if you want me to, but someone would have to call my mom and tell her. Oh, and here is your balloon back." The restaurant was silent. I got scared because everyone was staring at me in disbelief. I dropped the balloon and ran back out the door to my dad, who was rounding the corner.

He took me to a dirty motel-type room that had nothing in it but a bed, not even a bathroom. He said that it was his home. He lay down on the bed drunk and full. He said he was going to take a nap, and I was to lie down quietly next to him and sleep. I knew that it was time for me to be going home because it was getting dark. He wasn't allowed to keep me overnight. I kept trying to wake him. There was no phone in the room. After what felt like hours, I was able to get him to get up because I told him Mom would call the police if I didn't go home. He got up and said, "Stay here; I will be right back." I begged to go with, but he said not to and told me not to unlock the door. I was only preschool aged, but I somehow knew that danger lurked on the other side of the door, though I didn't know in what form. He returned after a while with a bottle in a brown bag and told me to come with him, that he was taking me home. I was so relieved.

Other visits weren't as dramatic. He would often take me to the local beauty school to get my hair cut short like a boy's even though I wanted long hair. One time the girl used a razor on my whole head, and it hurt so badly; my scalp was bleeding, and I started to cry. I looked like a boy when she was done. Then my dad sat me down and cut all of my fingernails and toenails so short that they all bled and were painful. I guess he had wanted a boy. Apparently, my mom did as well. She frequently placed a small mixing bowl on my head as a guide and used an old rusty scissors to cut my hair. I told her I looked like a boy and the kids at school made fun of me; I wanted long hair. She shrugged it off as she practically used a whole can of Aqua Net hairspray styling her feminine hairstyle.

Sometimes we would go looking for "treasure," as he would call it. He would have me walk around parks and lakes staring at the ground for hours, until the back of my naked neck was burned, looking for money or jewelry. When I got home, my mom would throw the "trash" away. One day he found little pieces of glass at the bus stop, and he insisted that he had found real diamonds that he was going to have put into a Black Hills gold ring he had won in a bet. He actually had the glass pieces put in, but he took the ring to a pawnshop to get money for alcohol. He wanted my mom to give him the money to get the ring out of hoc. She reluctantly did—her last sixty dollars—but the ring was already gone, and so was my mom's money.

He would often take me to the library when it was cold out. One time he stole a book from them; it was a Time Life book all about human sexual reproduction. He said, "Read this right away."

I replied, "I don't know how to read yet; Mom won't let me get shots for preschool."

"Well, look at the pictures and figure it out until you can read."

That was our first and last sex talk.

One day he took me to the state fair, complete with carnival games. I was so excited! He told me that he was a strong man who could throw a baseball and knock over all of the metal milk cartons in one toss. He was drunk as usual. He kept throwing the ball and missing. He was getting very angry. He was on his last try. I kept begging him to stop, telling him I didn't want the prize. He said we weren't leaving without him knocking down the cartons. He was yelling and causing a scene. I felt like the whole carnival stopped to stare. It was silent. He threw the ball so hard that he lost his balance, fell over the counter, and lay on the floor on the carny's side of the booth. Everyone gasped. He had missed all of the cartons. The worker felt so sorry for me he gave me a prize.

We left and approached the milk barn. All you can drink for 25 cents. We spent the rest of the day refilling our Dixie cups with fresh milk. He drank so many cups they ran out, and we left. When I got home, I showed my mom my prize that dad had won for me. It was a poster of Santa with green leaves stuffed into his bag to put under the tree. She told me to tear it up and throw it away. I was devastated and protested. She said that it was Santa delivering drugs under the tree, that it was inappropriate and to get rid of it. I took it to the trash and got sick from the overdose of milk.

He would call at all hours of the night, drunk, repeatedly threatening to come over. One night he told my mom that if she didn't wake me up so he could teach me the months of the year, he would come over and do it himself. She got me up and told me to pay attention and learn fast. She stood close by and tried to coach me along. I finally was able to recite all of the months of the year in order. Satisfied, he told me to put my mom back on the phone, and he let us go back to sleep.

My dad had been court ordered to Alcoholics Anonymous many times, but he refused to attend. My mom convinced him to check in to the Mayo clinic. She wrote some letters and got him accepted. We visited him every weekend. He had to go through a lot of electroshock therapy. Eventually they said that there was no hope for him; he had been drunk daily since he was 13, and he had a strong genetic predisposition and no desire to curb his drinking whatsoever, so he was released. I remember my mom saying, "If the Mayo clinic can't cure him, no one can."

His visits and calls were a constant stress for my mom and especially me. Over time, he would "no show" more and more frequently. I would stare out the window at 9:00 a.m. every Saturday like a puppy waiting for its owner to come home. I watched the people get off the bus right in front of our house. I would stand for hours waiting and worrying that he would show up. My mom started a new rule that if he was more than an hour late, he couldn't take me. If he was more than two hours late, we left, so if he showed up we wouldn't be there. When he showed up, he was always drunk. My mom said once, "She doesn't want to go with you, Jack; she is scared of you."

He turned to me and said, "Is that true, pal?" I was too terrified to answer, so I ran into the other room.

I was a disappointment to my dad. I didn't share in his love of nature or his one true passion, swimming. He showed up one hot, humid day in summer and announced that he was taking me to teach me how to swim. My dad had won medals in swimming in his youth. His participation on the YMCA swim team in his teen years had kept him in school long enough to graduate from high school in spite of his drinking.

He could swim like a fish in a pool, in the river, in the ocean; he didn't care. Many (especially him) have told me that he could have been an Olympic level swimmer had he pursued the sport properly in his youth. One thing he and I shared was a serious allergic response to many environmental factors. For me, this included chlorine; I was deathly allergic to it. He said, "The best way to learn how to swim is to get in and do it."

I was terrified by even the thought of going near the water. I had always been told to stay away from it, or I would drown since I didn't know how to swim. I wasn't even in school yet, and the community pool was full of big kids splashing around. My dad was clearly drunk and had a cigarette in his hand, as usual. The young lifeguard from the other side of the pool was watching my dad.

My dad picked me up, I started screaming, and he threw me in the deep end. My throat started to swell, I started to drown, and I was choking and trying to scream for help at the same time. I was dying. I saw my dad call off the lifeguard, who was posed to rescue me. My dad jumped in and pulled me out at the last second. I was sputtering water and gasping for breath. Everyone at the pool was silent and staring. No one moved. That was the end of my swim lessons. I got home, and my mom asked, "How was swimming?" to which I responded, "Dad tried to kill me."

The next time he picked me up, he decided that he needed new shoes. We took the bus to Kmart. He spent three hours trying on tennis shoes. He had taken every single adult men's pair of shoes; tried them on; walked around the store in them, leaving me sitting on the floor; and then would leave them on the floor for the employees to pick up. I fell asleep on the floor waiting for him. I was so bored, and I wanted to look at toys, but I knew better than to ask.

The announcement came over the loudspeaker that the store was closing, and we were to get in line to pay. I was so excited to be leaving. He had a blue pair of men's tennis shoes on. I said, "Let's go pay before they close." To which he responded, "No, I don't have any money; I just wanted to dream." We left. I call this "pretend shopping" now as I learned that my dad did a lot of that and that going shopping for him didn't mean what it meant to everybody else. When he told me we were going shopping, he meant we were going "dreaming."

Afterward, he had me sneak into a movie with him, which I didn't want to do. I just wanted to go home. He got up after a few minutes and said, "Stay here—don't leave your seat; I will be right back." The movie was almost over, and I was scared, not knowing what had happened to him. He finally sat down next to me with a bottle of beer in a brown bag, and he opened a pound of raw hamburger meat and asked me if I wanted any. I replied, "No, I would like popcorn."

"I am out of money—have hamburger."

"No thanks. I am not allowed to eat raw meat."

"Nonsense—it is good for you. Do you want some eggs?"

"Huh?"

He proceeded to pull out a dozen eggs in a carton, and he started cracking them open one by one and drinking them straight out of the shell.

"Dad, I am thirsty. Can I please have something to drink?"

"Sure, have an egg; it is good for you. Watch the movie."

One day he came to our house with a strange man with long hair who smelled like a skunk. He smiled at me, and the warmth of his smile made me feel safe. I was glad not to be alone with my dad, but I had never heard of my dad having a friend before. This man had a car and drove; I was so happy that we would not be hitchhiking. He introduced himself to my mom, and she called out to him, "Watch after Bobbi," to which he responded, "You have my word."

My dad couldn't drive; he'd had his license suspended long ago for multiple drunk driving offenses, and he was currently drunk, as usual. My dad demanded that the stranger take him to a remote farm to look at dogs. I knew that my dad had no money, and we weren't going shopping; we were going "dreaming."

After we looked for a long while at the giant dogs, my dad got in an intense argument with the dog owners. My guess is that after all these hours they found out he didn't have any money. I knew there was a serious problem. My dad started yelling. The stranger apologized to the dog owners. The dogs noticed the chaos and tension and started running in circles around me. The stranger said, "Bobbi, get in the car. I am taking you home to your mother."

I just wanted to go home, so I dutifully made a mad dash for the car. My dad lost it; he was so mad at me for obeying the hippie, stinky stranger. He told me to come back in the house. The stranger said, "Listen to me, Bobbi, and I will take you home." I bolted for the back seat. The stranger got in and said, "We are leaving your dad here to get his own ride; he will be fine."

The stranger peeled down the dusty road. We drove for a while, and he abruptly stopped the car. I was afraid he was going to leave me on the side of the road out in the country. He put the car in reverse and drove all the way back down the dirt road. My dad was walking down the road toward the car. The stranger yelled, "Get in!" They fought.

My dad turned to me and said, "Don't you EVER listen to someone else again!" I nodded in fear. "Okay, pal." We arrived home very late. My mom came out to the car in a panic, and the stranger told her what had happened. She thanked him repeatedly. I asked her if she was mad that I had listened to the stranger, who I learned had the name Steve, and she said that I did the right thing. She said, "We're done doing this." Soon afterward my dad announced that he was moving back to California for good.

He arrived for his final visit. I was sitting on the back porch eating raw herring. I am Swedish, Norwegian, English, and Irish; my Swedish heritage was prominent on my mom's side, and jars of herring were a staple in our house, my comfort food. My mom went inside the house and said, "Go say goodbye to your dad; you are not going to see him again for a very long time."

My dad stood staring at me in a way that made me feel uncomfortable, so I kept eating herring. He scooped me up in a big bear hug, jar in one hand and herring in the other. He gave me his typical sloppy wet kiss on the lips. My mouth was full with a big bite of fish. He said, "Goodbye, pal. I am going back to my home, the redwoods of California. Maybe you will come live with me there when you get older." I shrugged. "Bye, pal," I answered back.

He got into the car with Steve. I went back, sat on the porch, and continued to eat from the jar of herring. I was so happy. Happy about him leaving, and happy about having herring. My mom came to the door and asked through the porch screen, "Are you okay?"

To which I replied, "You betcha."

To which she responded, "Let's go get a Happy Meal." I felt as if life did not get any better than this.

I rarely heard from my dad after he returned to California. My dad made a claim for Social Security benefits, claiming that he was unfit to work. To prove his claim, he had to have a psychiatric evaluation, the results of which I found in his storage facility after he died.

This is a 52 year old white male who is divorced, from which he has one child. The patient has never worked. He is currently living in the woods, and he has no income. The patient has three concurrent prob-

lems. The patient suffers from extreme paranoia since he was walking down an alley with another man and three people came at him with iron pipes. The other man was killed, and he suffered a broken arm. Since that time he has been afraid of people, strangers especially, and almost anyone who vaguely resembles the persons who came at him in the alley. He is afraid of conversations. He feels like running and defending himself. He says that he can't think clearly, and he complains of feeling extreme fear. He gets very anxious if someone looks at him for too long a period. Since this time, he has been avoiding people of all kinds, and he has been living a very isolated existence in the woods. He says that he feels unable to control himself. He complains of intrusive and repeated episodes during which he has been around people that he has felt were going to get him. He complains of intense fear and anger, as well as a desire to kill people. At the same time, he complains of being detached from people. He can't stand to be around people anymore, and he feels overwhelmed with hatred of people. He has difficulty with concentration, and has had thoughts about death and suicide. He says that his behavior is very difficult to control, and he will begin screaming around people very easily and feels afraid that he is going to become angered to the point of having to harm someone.

The patient also complains of panic attacks, which are characterized by increased heart rate, shortness of breath, sweating, shaking, and fear of impending doom. These occur almost every day, and he feels he has to get a gun to defend himself. This has also occurred while drinking.

He describes himself as a person who has very few friends or social ties. He reports being close to his daughter (he had not had contact with me in years; I thought he was dead). *He has extreme difficulty with tender feelings of any kind. He believes in clairvoyance and telepathy. He has marked social isolation.*

He complains of the presence of a "power" around him which he has felt all of his life. He has experienced episodes of depersonalization reactions when he did not know who he was. He manifests very odd speech. He definitely is inadequate in his rapport on face-to-face contact. The patient also has a great deal of paranoia and extreme social anxiety.

The patient began drinking in junior high when he was 12. He would drink until drunk every time. He enlisted in the Navy, but was let go after two weeks due to being emotionally unstable. He was into German philosophy and metaphysics at the time. He wanted to study in the submarine reserves and was not able to learn what was going on there due to his mind trips and telepathy; he was unable to function.

The patient has multiple arrests regarding drinking. His manner is very anxious and fearful.

*Impression: This man is suffering from chronic Post Traumatic Stress Disorder. He is severely impaired at this time. He also has a panic disorder with panic attacks and agoraphobia. I believe that his alcohol abuse has covered up some of his panic symptoms. His alcohol abuse and dependence is very extreme. In **one year**, he has records of 83 admissions to a detox unit. In addition, this patient is suffering from a schizotypal personality disorder. I believe his personality has also been somewhat controlled by his alcohol use. This man is extremely impaired and unable to function in society. He is definitely unable to work.*

*Recommendations: I would not push this man! If he were forced to be in a situation of having to encounter people, I think there would be a potential for him to become violent. **As long as he is able to keep his distance from people, I don't think he is of any danger to others**.*

My dad was approved for Social Security benefits based on this report, probably for the better to keep him away from the public. He was ordered to attend Alcoholics Anonymous meetings, which he never did.

I thought it was interesting that he didn't share with the psychiatrist what had happened at another time prior to the alley attack when he was having an affair with a married woman. He was with her in a log cabin in the woods when her husband found them and shot my dad multiple times in the abdomen, including straight through his belly button out his spine. He was almost paralyzed for life. He was airlifted to San Francisco, where he almost died. He eventually came out of it but with an addiction to prescription painkillers.

He also left out the part about the main staple of his diet having been dog kibble. He lived on it for years. He always had an open bag of it ready to eat. He said that it had a lot of protein and didn't taste that bad. His other main staple was raw garlic that he would find. It is no wonder he never remarried or had more children, although he certainly tried to make that happen.

My dad sponsored three young Filipino girls in their teens. He sent his whole Social Security check to these young women. He sponsored them through agencies that focused on feeding children, but my dad had ulterior motives; he wanted them to come to the United States and for one of them to be his wife. I guess he was casting a big net just in case.

He contacted me once after being absent for many years and asked me for $12,000 to sponsor one of them to come to the US. He had her write me and ask for the money as well. When I declined, he became very angry and left me messages ranting about what an awful daughter I was. This went on for many years. He sent pictures to these women of himself in his twenties. He also told them he was rich. One went on to grow up and get married and have a child in her country, and he still tried to bring her and her son here to be his "new family."

One of them actually came to the United States, never met my dad, and married someone else. Of course, that was my fault as well, since I didn't give him the money and agree to sign to sponsor her. These women would have been surprised if they had arrived and found out that my dad was in his seventies, homeless, living in the redwoods, and sustained by dog food. He never gave my mom or me a dime in our lives, and he was sending all of his money to these women. That was a hurtful reality, which I still struggle with.

After my dad left Minnesota when I was about four, I seldom heard from him. When I did, it was in spurts of time when he seemed to be doing better, and usually my only contact was through his letters to me that I answered with my own letters. He likened himself to a modern-day Thoreau. I am so thankful that I kept all of his letters, even though my mom and I were transient, and that he had kept all of my letters that I recovered from his storage after his death. Letter writing is a dying art form, and with it will die the history and knowledge of where we came from. These letters give me a window into a time and man that I call my dad.

Dear Pal,

I am living in the redwoods; it's a very nice place. The redwoods are where I belong; I guess you could say, I like it here. I don't like living next door to anyone. I live alone except for the birds and some forest critters. A skunk came to visit me yesterday. I was busy so I didn't have the time to get acquainted with him. I am pretty sure he/she will be back. I will leave food out for the animals and pretty soon, I will be the most popular human on this hilltop. Later on, I will send you a picture of my new friends. Animals are God's children. Something we should not forget. Animals thought my dad (your grandpa) was god. Your grandpa had an unusual affinity with animals. They really responded to him.

To live apart from nature is to live apart from one's self. I respect nature, and I am still innocent to believe that this earth is the only real home I will ever have. I really love plants and animals.

I found a Doberman puppy. I have named him Sam. I beat him with a switch and a fly swatter. I know I am mean, heartless and cruel, and I will probably go to hell because of it, but the way I hear it, there are so many down there now that there may not be any room for yours truly. I kind of like my dog. He is beautiful, and one of a kind with green eyes. Some people say we look like father and son. He was run over by a car, so I had a leg splint put on him.

*Dogs wait in the same place for someone they love, always hoping that someday they will return. Dogs are very loyal **people**. I see from the picture you sent me that you have a dog, and you humanize it, don't do that, and remember it is a dog.*

I love you pal, Dad

Dear Pal,

You know honey; I have never run into anyone like me. I am humble, handsome, and extremely intelligent.

*Remember that it is always better to have **lived** than never to have **lived** at all. Be kind to yourself always. Choose your friends wisely for all others will not always be kind to you. Live your own life, because no one can live it for you. Life is both mysterious and beautiful. Be on good terms with this world in which you find yourself. When you have a problem, it is well to remember that it is best to live in the solution rather than living in the problem.*

Your happiness in life will depend on making wise decisions. Be honest with yourself always, be willing to accept whatever limitations you discover about yourself, and go from there. Happiness and love are twins—they go together, and are one and the same.

Remember that a creative life is in its own reward, and of all forms of art, the art of living is the most difficult, but also the most satisfying. I want to be able to say that this one life I live will not have been in vain.

Travel—I guess maybe I would like for you to live the life for me that I could never live.

Leave alcohol alone—and other drugs and you will have a good life. Some people can drink a few drinks and know when they have had enough. I was never one of those people. I can't even drink one drink. If I do, I am in deep trouble. I am chemically and biologically unable to drink only one drink. I had enough problems with botanical drugs too in the past. It has destroyed a lot of lives.

Basically, if I don't write you for three or four months, then you will know something has happened to me. I have died.

Your dad,

Jack Robbins, Esq.

(He was a self-proclaimed attorney.)

Dear Pal,

*I am sorry I am running a little late honey; it has been a **year** since my last letter. Happy belated birthday!*

Thank you for the Swiss army knife you sent me, it is very sharp, and I can shave with it.

I have been busy this last year; sometimes I take off for the desert or mountains. Between books and prospecting in the river, my life is good and getting better all the time.

I read a lot. My favorite book is Walden by Thoreau. I also like Henry Miller and Alan Watts. The preface to Tropic of Cancer by Karl Shapiro is swell as well.

I have learned that it is not wise to loan out your books to others, no matter who they are. Why? Because you will most likely never get them back. I have had to learn this slowly.

Well, I have to get back to my prospecting. I just want to say thank you for lifting the lid on the coffin of my depression. I have sent you a series of letters that I have written to you over the past year and am just now getting around to mailing. I don't like to go into town. The letters are all interconnected, and all together, they will form a book. It was not my intention to write a book of letters—but this is what has been happening. I love to write, almost as much as I love being around books."

Love,

Your pal,

Dad

Typically, the letters were written on scraps of paper, and a trinket, like a piece of driftwood, a shell, or a rock that he had drawn eyes on, was usually enclosed.

I thought of the Bible verse where Jesus says, "Would any of you give your hungry child a stone if the child asked for some bread?" My dad would, and he would tell me to make stone soup.

As my dad aged and got into his upper seventies, he had to make the trip into town more often. Not only did he want to mail money to the women in the Philippines, but also he was frequently ill. He would stumble into town wrapped in his blankets, looking like a crazy mountain man. At times, he would sleep in a sleeping bag on the sidewalk to avoid the walk back into the redwoods at night in the rain. He also lived for a period in an abandoned van, and then an abandoned car. He was a hoarder and kept everything he found, so he didn't have room to sleep, let alone sit in the vehicles, which were illegally parked and were eventually towed.

He was spending time in Arcata, located in Humboldt County in Northern California, which is rife with homelessness, largely due to drug addiction. He befriended the local homeless and spent time getting meals at the senior center and going to his doctor's appointments for his teeth, eyes, feet, . . . and the list goes on. He was always insisting he was dying of a rare disease that he had read about. He was known to be a hypochondriac and became a well-known character by the locals in the town.

He had continued to smoke daily since his childhood, and it had wreaked havoc on his lungs. He developed a terrible cough, exacerbated by living outside in a very cold environment. He was about six feet tall and looked like a walking skeleton. He had long, shaggy gray hair, and no teeth. In his youth, he had won a contest and been in the local newspaper for having perfect teeth without braces. Years of biting off beer bottle caps and a lack of personal hygiene eventually led to him losing all of his teeth.

A social worker was made aware of him, and she placed him in the local homeless mission. He hated following the rules of the mission, like getting up and out on demand, no smoking inside, etc. He hadn't slept in a real bed since he was a child, and he was put into a bunk bed. He fell out of the bed and fractured his hip. The social worker called me apologetically. I felt for her, as she was just trying to help. At least now he was in a hospital getting daily meals and being monitored.

When he was released, he was put in a halfway house, although he was nowhere near "half way." His drinking was continuous, as it served as a painkiller for his hip and helped him cope with having to be around people so much. I was so happy that he was in a home where he was being monitored and fed, but his alcoholic tendencies made him impossible to deal with. He frequently fell down the stairs drunk and caused problems for the other residents and the managers. His hip bounced back like a spring chicken, and he went back to his preferred lifestyle in the woods with frequent trips to town.

In 2017, Northern California had some of its strongest rains in years. My dad had hepatitis, as well as pneumonia that wreaked havoc on his already fragile lungs. He went to an emergency room, where they airlifted him by helicopter to the nearest city, about 100 miles away. The hospital determined that there was nothing they could do for him, but now he was many miles from his redwood home. My dad, ever the conniving genius, knew he was going to be released, lied and said that he had fallen and hit his head while in their care (with no witnesses), so they had better keep him for monitoring, which they did. This bought him a lot more time.

We spent time talking on the phone, but he had such limited air capacity that his breathless speech was usually unintelligible. I told him that I was sorry if I ever did anything to hurt him and that I forgave him for anything he did to me, to which he took huge offense. He mustered up enough oxygen to yell through a whisper, "What do I have to be sorry for? I was the perfect father!"

I asked him if he had any last wishes, as the hospital staff informed me that the end was near, and he was in full knowledge and acceptance of the fact. He said he wanted to be cremated and wanted me to clean out his storage facilities that he paid for with his Social Security check. I assured him that I would take care of everything, as requested. I asked him where he thought he was going to go after he died, to which he responded rather loudly, "To infinity and beyond!" He had no more air to speak at that point; gasping for air, he hung up the phone. He died not long afterward.

My husband drove me up north with dogs in tow to pick up his remains. I was given a bag of his personal belongings and a trash bag that had in it the dirty, torn clothes he had worn to the emergency room. The local homeless shelter wanted to have a memorial for him, at the request of the locals.

Since my dad's life had been outside the norm, it should have been no surprise to me that his death would have been as well, although it was. My dad's remains were in the box, but the memorial was way outside the box. The kind staff served coffee and desserts. The local homeless were clamoring at the door, trying to get their hands on the food and drink.

An uncharacteristic, overwhelming feeling came over me as I looked out at the table full of guests, including homeless, senior citizens and mental health professionals who had known my dad. It was a feeling of intense anger, which, I am sure, masked pain. Here I was delivering a eulogy for a man who had never approved of me. He had felt that I was dumb for pursuing a formal education; "overweight," as he wrote all over my favorite picture of myself that I had sent him; foolish for being a Christian; stupid for going to work and having a career; and the list goes on.

My dad had physically, psychologically, emotionally, spiritually, verbally, and economically abused my mom, his mom, his dad, and me. I had no idea of the extent to which this had happened until after the fact, when his storage was cleaned out.

My dad had destroyed everyone and everything in his life that he supposedly cared about, from his beloved redwood trees that he had helped his dad chop down in his youth to his relationships with his family and even to his doppelganger dog.

My dad lived until he was 82. Some of my students never made it to adulthood, and they were so full of potential. My best friend, who was my angel on earth, not just for me but for so many, barely saw her forties. My mom, who changed the lives of so many through education, only made it to 68. She never had a eulogy or a memorial service, so why should this man be honored or remembered favorably?

It was then that I asked God for peace and strength to forgive and forget, to let go, and let God use me to minister to those who were grieving the loss of my dad, even though I wasn't. I had grieved not having a dad when I was a child, and I was over it. Secretly I had prayed that he would die earlier in life, as I just couldn't take him anymore. I was there to eulogize a stranger who in my eyes had died long ago.

God took this mess and turned it into my message. In the end, I was blessed by the experience. I heard stories of my dad that I would have never known, and they made me smile. A Good Samaritan a week prior to his hospitalization took him to dinner, had his hair cut short, and took his picture, which is a priceless treasure to me now.

There was the story of how someone offered to take him to coffee to warm him. He could have had a gourmet coffee shop, but he chose 7-11 instead. A young homeless man was thankful that my dad showed him the ropes of living on the streets. A man knew him in his youth and spoke of his desire to be physically fit. He couldn't believe that my dad ever smoked a day in his life based on his zeal for health.

If he only knew! I was named after that man who was almost 90, and we finally got to meet. My dad got into a car recently with a woman who had left her car door unlocked and scared her to death, but he hadn't realized it was the wrong car and got out right away. All of these stories I will cherish in my heart. I didn't have any heartwarming stories to share, but I was happy to know that others did.

My husband and I cleaned out his two stuffed storage facilities. My dad was a purveyor of all things old. Boxes of books, coins, stamps, records, postcards, none of which had any monetary value, filled his space alongside boxes of pornography that he would try to resell at the local swap meet during lean times over his lifetime. There was a box full of the mail I had sent him over the years, including every birthday and Father's Day card that I labored over choosing. At the time, Hallmark didn't acknowledge that not all fathers are "the greatest." I stuck with the one solitary card annually that read plainly, "Happy Father's Day."

There were letters from the Philippines. There were letters from his dad begging him to stop drinking for my sake. There were letters from my mom begging him to stop beating her when I was a baby. There was his psych report, military and medical records from his past. Why would a person keep such incriminating evidence? I believe that everything was divinely preserved to one day help me put the pieces of the mysterious puzzle of my dad together. Well, maybe not the used sex toys, but everything else.

I found a safe deposit key that we took to the bank. I can no longer say that he died penniless, or that he never gave me one penny, as it had exactly one penny in it.

My husband and I released some of his ashes into the ocean by Trinidad Bay, a place he had loved. We also released some in the redwoods by Avenue of the Giants, near his childhood residence, and in the forest that he considered home. We found a redwood tree stump to pour the ashes next to. As I looked at the rings of life, I remembered sitting with him in my front yard as a very small child.

I reflected on what I learned from my dad. He kept popping in and out of my life, giving me a sense of uncertainty, which I believe promoted a lack of trust in men to be present when needed. When he was present, I feared him, which in turn led me to be a peacekeeper and a "perfect" child to keep him content. I found myself in my youth only befriending those that came from homes with single mothers, as we could really bond over our life experiences. This in turn led to even fewer role models of what a "typical" family looked like and how it functioned. I didn't understand what role each person in a family played.

Due to my dad's choices, I had to start babysitting as a child to make ends meet, get my first real job at 15, and work many hours on top of school due to our food and shelter uncertainty. My peers were able to focus on school and not spend their time looking for quarters on the street to have a scoop of Thrifty ice cream to get some food in each day. I could have gone straight into a university instead of working and going to college full time for so many years.

As I look back, I realize that I sought male approval at an early age, as I had never experienced it and longed for love from a male. I married young and naïve, due to the lack of a dad's love and approval in my life. My dad should have been a mirror for me growing up in which I could see myself and could discover who I was as I related to males, but this all had to be learned later in life, which has put me at a disadvantage in relationships.

If I would have had a dad, perhaps other males in life would not have victimized me, as they would have known I was protected, and I wouldn't have been such easy prey in my youth. If my dad had been present, I wouldn't have been victimized in my stepdad's house, as I would have had a dad's protective nature to shield me. My mom wouldn't have had to work so much if he had been around, so I would have known her better as well. She wouldn't have been the emotionally wounded, exhausted person with whom I grew up.

My mom taught me how to live, and my dad taught me how not to live. This in itself has value. Some things he taught me by modeling them, and others he taught me through negligence. By example, he taught me that a person could live simply; you can't take it with you. He taught me to love knowledge for knowledge's sake, not so I could chase after diplomas or career advancement. He taught me to appreciate nature even though I am a city girl. By disregard, he taught me to value family, to want whatever it is you have. He taught me to not drink or use drugs due to my genetic predisposition. He taught me to believe in a higher power than myself.

To me, a man's role is to be a teacher, leader, provider, and protector of his family. My dad was none of these, so my mom spent her life trying to do double duty. Some people are not meant to be married or have children, and I will always respect the fact that once he figured that out he never remarried or had more children; to this end, I give him credit. It may be that he learned from that mistake. The absence of a dad from my life developed in me a reliance on God to be my Father in a way that I would never otherwise have known. My Father in heaven became my provider, protector, leader, and teacher from an early age. I am glad that my dad left to make room for my Father to fill that Jesus-sized void in my life. God truly turned fear into strength and ashes into beauty.

As my dad's ashes made way to the ground, all I could think was, "Good luck, Dad, as you enter infinity and beyond; off you go into the wild blue yonder. I wish you would have listened to *me*, pal—you should've listened to *me*."

Life lessons from my dad (Jack):
1. How not to live. This in itself has value.
2. Live simply, you can't take it with you.
3. Love knowledge for knowledge's sake.
4. Appreciate nature.
5. Value family. Want what you have.
6. Don't drink or use drugs. Know your limits, and stay within them.
7. Believe in a higher power than myself.
8. A man's role is to provide, protect, lead, and teach. If you're a man, do those things for your family; if you are a woman, support men in this endeavor.
9. Don't try to assuage your guilt by giving handouts to the homeless on the street; give only generous hand-me-ups to agencies that systematically assist people in need. Our laziness is not solving the problem; it is only adding to it by enabling this dangerous behavior to continue.

5.
Zoe and Zorro's Box

As I open the fifth box, a pink plastic bin, and pull out a tiny dress, my mind wanders back in time not too long ago, as this is my freshest and deepest grief, and it evokes in me a deep visceral feeling of loss.

In my mind's eye, I picture the story of me in my first and only fashion show that I took part in at the school where I was a professional school counselor. It was to raise money for student scholarships. We were to invite friends and family to model with us. I brought my adorable fur baby Zoe, adorned in this black and cheetah print dress to match the school mascot. I was dressed in all black, and my dog, Zorro, was riding in the dog stroller that I pushed down the runway. Lady Gaga's "Romance" blared over the speaker. "Rah rah ah-ah-ah! Ro mah ro-mah-mah!" That was our cue. Zoe was so small; I held her in my right arm and pushed Zorro with my left hand. The audience went wild as Zoe stole the show with her big brown junior mint eyes. She loved the attention, being in the spotlight, the loud music, and the cheers coming from the audience. She started bobbing her head to the deafening sounds. I was so excited and turned around so fast Zorro almost went flying out of the stroller. We were on the catwalk where the then popular television show *Glee* filmed regularly on our stage. I thought,

"*Glee* ain't got nothin' on us!" Zoe was a natural; she belonged in the spotlight. We went backstage, hugged, and took pictures to remember our special moment of stardom together.

There are many of Zoe's clothes in this bin, as each one evokes a memory. Each item, an emotion. There are also a lot of photos and some random papers, as well as some of her favorite toys that I just can't part with, and even her favorite bottle and bowl.

On April 16, 2005, I fell in love. I was 36. A rule follower by nature, I knew that I couldn't adopt a dog; I was a renter, and there was a strict policy against pets. I loved where I lived and had no plans of leaving my affordable, safe housing. I had had cats in my youth. Skeezix was my first pet, followed by Chasse. They were aloof but loved; they were . . . cats. My stepbrother had a dog that I cohabitated with in my youth. She was a nice cocker spaniel mix named Missy, but she wasn't mine, and I didn't want to be in that house, so no bonding took place with her whatsoever. After all, she was a dog, not a person. Although I loved animals in general, I didn't love them enough to be a vegetarian or to run into the ocean to save a sea creature.

I wasn't looking for it, but it was truly love at first sight. I went to the America's Family Pet Expo just to get some fresh air and exercise at the fairgrounds. Although I had no interest in adopting a pet, I felt compelled all of a sudden to walk through the dog adoption area. There she was, a Chihuahua/Jack Russell terrier mixed mutt. Only a year and half old, with stitches from just having been spayed. She looked at me, and our eyes locked. She looked so hopeful, and I felt so happy. She shook with excitement at the certainty that I was her new mom. I shook with the knowledge that I had to have her, . . . and I couldn't.

I bolted for the bathroom. I tried to calm down, but I couldn't. Even though I was not prone to anxiety or panic attacks, I started to have one right there in the stall. I prayed that she would not be there, so I wouldn't have a chance to adopt her when I walked out the door because I knew that I had to be obedient and not risk my current living situation, which was otherwise perfect for me. Concurrently, I prayed that she would still be there, as I knew I couldn't go on living happily without her, and in the same breath that she would not be there, because I knew I had no place to live with her. I had mixed feelings; I was sweating and shaking out of control. The adrenaline was coursing through my body. I thought I was going to have a heart attack.

I threw my fleece before God. If she was still there, I was taking her home, and I would figure out the rest later. If she was not there, I had to trust God that it was not meant to be. I exited the restroom and turned the corner. I opened my eyes and looked anxiously at the area where she had been fenced in. She was gone. Did someone else adopt her? I felt like I was going to die at the moment. I started to hyperventilate. Then the volunteer rounded the corner with her in her arms. She had just had a bathroom break! I called over the volunteer and took my fur baby into my arms. The worker took our picture together, and we left on our adventure called life.

First mission, shop until we drop at the pet fair. I bought her one of everything they sold. I could barely fit it all in the car. She even decided on her own clothes. She chose a pink shirt by literally jumping up and knocking it off the hanger. Aha! Her favorite color is the same as mine—pink! Technically, I had rescued her, but in reality she saved me. Life had been filled with so many hardships and disappointments. I guess God knew that I needed someone to love and to *be* loved. My fur baby gave me new hope for a brighter future. I named her Zoe after the all-female contemporary Christian singing group that I had just seen in concert. Zoe in the original Greek means "Spirit-filled, abundant life" and that is exactly what Zoe and I were going to experience side by side. I had a new lease, and she had a new leash, on life. It was a divine pairing.

I marveled at the fact that we met in Costa Mesa. Me hailing from Long Beach, her from way out in San Bernardino. We were brought together in an unlikely city and time. She had long, muscular, beautiful legs, brownish/auburn short fur. A white star (my favorite symbol) adorned her side and her bottom. Her tail was in the shape of a question mark. She was one of a kind. Truly, the most beautiful dog I had ever laid eyes on. She clearly had a previous owner, as she already knew how to fetch the newspaper, which was bigger than she was. She knew many tricks and was perfectly obedient.

I wondered if her previous owner had died. She was clearly loved and cared for. Did Zoe think of her owner and miss her? I wish I had seen her when she was born, as a tiny puppy. She wasn't very big even now, so I bet she was adorable. Was her previous owner sitting somewhere crying over her picture? The thought of it made me sad, so I vowed to never consider it again. She had been the favored dog in the shelter, where they had named her Michelle. I am sure Zoe was happy to be away from the desert heat and now living near the ocean breeze.

I had bought a crate bed for her and put her in it the first night. I turned out the light; ten seconds later I heard a faint whimper, then a little whine. It broke my heart. I opened the crate, and she jumped up onto my bed, where she remained for the next ten years. The next day I donated the crate.

I called the owner of my rental to let her know that I had adopted a dog, and she said I would need to move. Even though I could not afford it, I prayed for a miracle, and I bought a condo, essentially a $300,000 dog house, complete with open air atrium on the second floor so Zoe could come in and out at her will and sunbathe on her sunlit patio complete with real sod grass that I hauled upstairs weekly—and her own fire hydrant. The sign on the door had a ceramic image of Zoe that read, "Su casa, es mi casa." In addition, a flag that proclaimed, "A Chihuahua and her staff live here." It's true; the home became the Condo de Chihuahuas overnight.

One morning when we were still getting to know each other, I told her we were going on a car ride to Starbucks. She looked at me with an expression I had never seen before. Her eyes widened in disbelief. I said, "Zoe, do you like Starbucks?" She jumped up and ran in circles like I had never seen before. She went "wild chi" on me. I said, "Zoe, I want a mocha."

At the word "mocha," she jumped up onto me and started licking me in a frantic mode. I felt like Fred Flintstone being attacked by Dino when he came home from work. "Zoe, do you like mochas?" I repeated mocha over and over, and each time she stared at me, shook, and went crazier. That was it! Her name had been "Mocha!" I should have guessed it, as she was mocha colored with white spots that looked like whipped cream. Now she had three names: "Zoe Mocha Michelle." She responded to all of them.

We went everywhere together. We always dressed alike. An outfit for every occasion. When we went to Taco Bell, she wore her "Yo Quiero Taco Bell" shirt picturing the Chihuahua that had made the phrase popular. I was a first-time fur mom, so I made my share of mistakes. I gave her too many treats, so much so that her clothes started to get tight on her. I took her for ice cream, which I didn't know some can't tolerate, and she got sick. I let her eat avocados with me. She loved them. I didn't know that they could be harmful. At a boutique I bought her treats that she was allergic to; she broke out into terrible hives, and I had to rush her to the emergency vet for treatment. Zoe was always so forgiving. She didn't judge my lack of pet parenting skills.

We frequented all of the local pet stores. She rode in the cart and would wag her tail when she saw something that she liked. I chose for her pink boots that she did not like, but she tolerated them for the professional photo shoot. She had a designer dog necklace that cost more than any of my jewelry. It had a pink, plastic Chihuahua head charm on it and a charm that read "Chiwowwow," which is exactly what I said when I found out the price! It was made of plastic, and I used up the credit on my plastic so she could have it. No regrets—seeing Zoe in that necklace was priceless.

She would sit up on her back legs in a position to get taller so she could check everything out. She would look around at the items in a way that would put any meerkat to shame. She could jump five feet from a standing position up into my arms with me standing. This was very entertaining to those who witnessed it.

We were invited to dog parties. During one dog birthday party we attended she sat in her "meerkat" position at the dining room table on a chair. She ate the cake just like a human (sans hands) right off the plate in her China doll dress. She didn't make a mess at all. Everyone cackled at the sight, and she looked over to me like, "What is everyone laughing at?"

She had so many expressions. She would stick her face out from under her blanket that had frayed edges to reveal her head that looked like it was adorned in dreadlocks, and then she would get a big Bob Marley grin on her face. This became a nightly ritual to garner a laugh.

In the mornings, she would open one eye and look at me to see if I was awake. She would stay in bed until I was ready to get up. She never got up at night. If she didn't want me to sleep in and she was bored, she would shake like a leaf, and if I turned over to go back to sleep, she would make a quiet little "mmm" sound like Marge Simpson when she was upset with Homer, right before she would say his name. I would pat her on the head, and, more reliable than a snooze alarm, exactly thirty minutes later we would do it all over again.

She loved to pose for photos. She would freeze in a coquettish pose. She would make faces for selfies. She even photo bombed other people's pictures; she would run up to the camera and completely cover the other people in the photo, and then she would grin and run off.

She loved to open presents, even those that were not her own. She would stick her head into the gift bags, pull out the contents, and run around with glee. She loved toys, especially those that required her to pull out objects from a holder or box. She would play dog puzzles and would always find the treats in just a few seconds. Each one I bought for her was too easy. She would tear open a dog toy and pull out the plastic squeaker. She would run to drop it off at my feet to get her prize treat.

Zoe was so brilliant that I wanted to use her paw for my cell phone touch ID so she could call 911 for me if there were an emergency. I bought special flashcards for dogs. She learned to "read" the commands on the cards and do the tricks at the sight of the card. She had about a handful of "sight words."

Like everyone, the groomers loved her. They painted her tail in red, white, and green for Cinco de Mayo. They gave her candy cane striped nails for Christmas.

She would always dress thematically, but one of her favorite dresses was black with her face in faux diamond bling on it. It was an exact likeness. She wore it with her pink pearl necklace. She knew it was party time whenever she wore her pearls.

She loved it when I would sing and dance with her in my arms. We did everything together. She did "downward dog" next to me as I did my cool down stretch daily after my morning workout DVD. She knew the daily routine. She helped carry the "sock balls" to the bedroom and would even drop them in the right place in the dresser drawer. She could pick up her toys and drop them back into her toy bin. When work was done, she would curl up under my right arm, where she fit perfectly, and take a nap. I would read lying on my stomach on the bed, and she would jump up and gently knead my back to give me a massage after a long day.

Life was not easy for me, with multiple losses over a short period. I would talk to Zoe and tell her my worries. She would look at me and listen attentively. This would be followed by a knowing expression that always said, "Don't worry; we will cross that bridge together when we get to it." And cross bridges we did, literally and figuratively. She indeed helped me cross the challenging bridges of life. From moving to a new condo to foreclosing on the condo to three more moves, to the deaths of my best friend, mom, dad, and ten of my students, to the essential "loss" of my daughter that drove a wedge into our relationship, to going to school for my doctorate, having major surgery, and a myriad of other issues too lengthy to list here. Zoe was always by my side; her very presence encouraged me to go on another day. Zoe loved life, and she brought rainbow colors and joy to my otherwise dark and stormy existence.

I prayed daily for a good Christian man to come into my life. It dawned on me about four months after adopting Zoe that she might like to have a life partner. I set out to find Zoe a husband to share her life with.

I knew it would take some time and effort to find a boy dog as handsome, brilliant, sweet, and talented as Zoe. I checked online daily. We lived next door to a new ASPCA, which made the search easier. One day I walked in, and there he was: a small black Chihuahua with a little bit of white under his nose and on his paws, with what looked like a tiny black moustache drawn under his nose. He was about the same size and age as Zoe. He had just arrived, so I couldn't take him home until he had been cleared and the shelter was sure that no one was looking for him. His big brown eyes met mine; he was looking lost, and I was feeling found.

He started pawing at the cage to get out. I promised him I would come back and get him out once he was cleared. I had a dream about him that night. I woke up in a start, which I never do. I said aloud, "Name him Zorro." This wasn't altogether surprising, as the movie *Zorro* was my favorite, and the dog was a mix between Chihuahua and fox terrier. *Zorro* means fox in Spanish. He had big brown eyes like Antonio Banderas, so it all made sense. Besides, Zoe and Zorro just sounded right.

The volunteers called me to set up a bark and greet. They informed me that Zorro had to also pass a test for me to be able to take him home. After about 15 minutes, the volunteers emerged. "Is it kismet?" I asked. "Hardly—they are both dominant dogs. We will allow you to adopt him, but know that it will be challenging." I thought, *What relationship isn't?*

"I am up for the challenge," I boldly proclaimed. "Where do I sign?" When I got up to the adoption area, a man offered me money to let him take my new fur baby home for his mom. He said, "That is exactly the dog my mom is looking for." I said, "I am sorry; he's spoken for." He replied, "He looks like a Zorro; that is what my mom was going to name him."

I knew he had been aptly labeled. The shelter had called him Stanley, a big name for a little guy. Zoe and I whisked him off quickly to the groomer and purchased some shampoo and dog perfume from Paris to make sure he never smelled like the city pound again. As we entered our condominium, a little girl about three years old said to her mom, "That dog looks like Stanley!" The mom said, "You're right, he does." The mom kept walking, and the little girl kept staring. I was perplexed by her comment and the mom's reaction. I decided to let it go, as I knew in my heart that Zorro was my legal fur baby, and I would never let anyone take him away. I had already fallen head over heels for this little guy.

The days that followed were filled with shopping for clothes for him so he didn't have to be seen naked when his wife was so well dressed. He tolerated Zoe and my doting over him surprisingly well. Zoe had a poodle skirt costume, so Zorro had to be Elvis with a big pompadour wig to match. For every one of her Princess shirts, he had a Prince one to match.

They had a wedding ceremony where Zoe dressed in a white gown and Zorro wore a tuxedo. They exchanged a Tiffany dog toy diamond ring and had professional photos.

I took them to the Blessing of the Animals because we needed all of the blessings we could get. Zoe insisted on drinking the blessed water that the priest was using to put on their heads. They were such a hit at the blessing that they were videotaped and used in the next year's commercial for the event. A little girl approached me. She was staring at Zorro. She said, "That is the cutest dog I have ever seen in my life!" She was right; I had the cutest boy and girl dogs on the planet, and I am sure I wasn't biased in any way.

Zorro was definitely all boy. He liked to get dirty. He liked to chase squirrels and possums, even though they were bigger than he was. He definitely had a Napoleon complex. He barked nonstop at every dog that came within a mile radius of him. The bigger the dog, the louder the bark. It made it near impossible to take him out or on a walk. He even barked in his sleep when he wasn't snoring.

I enrolled them in two obedience classes (one at the park, and one at the pet store), which Zoe took offense to, but she could have been valedictorian. They both graduated with flying colors. Zorro even won most improved, thanks to the trainer's help. She said he needed a gentle choke chain, which I tried, but he had a seizure while in it. I panicked, as I thought I was going to lose him. Then she said to spray him with water when he barked. I dutifully took the water bottle wherever we went. Zorro was soaked . . . and barked even louder. I vowed to let him just be him and bark as he willed. No more obedience training.

Zorro wasn't just a barker; he was a chewer. He chewed through plugged-in electrical cords, through wood on doors, even through carpeting. It did not matter to him that he had every chew toy known to dog; he wanted a bigger challenge.

One day I came home and he had chewed through the wall; he was stuck halfway through the heater, and he was still barking! I would like to say that Zoe looked worried, but she looked more entertained than anything. I gently pulled him out of the wall heater. He had chewed through the electrical wires in the heater. It made for a long, cold winter.

One time I came home from work, and he had chewed through the floor level air conditioner and escaped into the backyard. That made for a long, hot summer. People would say he looked a little like a cat, but he had many more than nine lives—more like ninety.

One day he had a thick, red substance all over his paws; I was sure he had gotten into something and had injured himself. I scooped him up in a panic and ran for the car to take him to the emergency vet, only on closer inspection to find that he had stomped on some berries. He had severe allergies and had to take medication, and yet he never seemed to get drowsy or be adversely affected. He would get the "zoomies" nightly and go running around like he was a sprinter, bumping into everything head first, doing a cartoon-character-like flip, and jumping up and continuing to run full speed ahead. I would chase him around the house trying to catch him to calm him down.

He dug under the bedroom dresser to get the ant bait and ended up chewing through the plastic and consuming some of the poison. I called animal poison control; I dutifully kept their number on the refrigerator. I didn't realize that the ant bait had peanut butter in it, and Zorro was a peanut butter junkie. Another crisis averted, as he survived.

Zorro had a strong-willed personality. One minute he would be licking my feet to show me his love and appreciation, and then I would want to take a picture of him. I would say, "Smile, Zorro!" He would consistently respond with sticking out his tongue at me. Zoe would get jealous and photo bomb the shot. I bought him a T-shirt that said "I have issues." Zoe got the one that said "Therapist." Zoe asked for a divorce; I declined and said to give it time.

In his youth, Zorro wasn't just a barker and a chewer; he was a runner. One day he was out back with Zoe for a moment, and I ran to get my phone. All of a sudden, I heard kids yelling at my front door. The meter reader had just stopped by and didn't close the gate latch all the way, and my dogs were out. I grabbed up Zoe, but Zorro was nowhere to be found. I lived on a very busy street, and he was so small. I prayed and tried not to panic. I was in my pajamas and barefoot. I grabbed Zoe's leash and said, "Zoe, go find Zorro!"

She got a big smile on her face and darted as fast as she could to the left. I ran behind her; as she had such strong Jack Russell legs, she could run like the wind. My feet were being burned and cut by the pavement, but I didn't care; I had to have my fur baby back. I had my cell phone. We were about a block away, and I was yelling Zorro's name. The neighbors were coming outside to see what was going on.

My phone rang. A woman had found Zorro. Her daughter saw that he was alone with a collar. I am so glad that I had his name and phone number embroidered into his collar, and he also had a microchip. He was found about a block to the right. He had crossed the busy street! I looked at Zoe, and Zoe looked at me with the biggest grin I had ever seen. She had purposely thrown me off in hopes of getting the divorce she had always wanted. I hugged my baby and rewarded the girl and her mom. Once again, God had saved Zorro.

I remember in high school when I went over to my friend's house, her mom had a little white dog that had bows in her hair and her nails painted. I had never seen anything like that. My friend commented, "That's my mom's dog; she loves her more than me." I remember feeling so confused about how this mother humanized her dog. The woman died of breast cancer not long afterward, and her dog was more comfort to her than her wayward daughter was. Oddly, now I fully understand. I know this is hard to understand unless you have personally experienced this unique bond. Although I don't have multiple children, I would guess that this is similar to a parent loving all of her children, but really liking some more than others, due to a special connection.

Zoe took on Zorro as her own little "pet" project. She taught him how to lift his leg (even though she was a female) to pretend to urinate out back to get a treat reward. In reality, they weren't doing anything but going through the motions. The neighbor even approached me and asked if I was in on their joke. I was. When Zoe had to really go, she did a handstand so as to be sure not to get her paws wet. I figured if they were so smart as to "act" for me, they still deserved a treat.

We didn't go for many walks, as my little dogs thought they were pit bulls. We walked once around our block, and a German shepherd got out from a gate and attacked us. I was terrified of German shepherds, as I had witnessed two "well trained" German shepherd attacks on children in my youth. My dogs decided to "protect" me. I grabbed them into my arms as the beast lunged toward me. My dogs barked and tried to get at him. I screamed for help. The owners came out and said, "Oh, the gate must have been unlocked." Nothing worse than irresponsible large dog owners. Thus ended our neighborhood walks.

Nonetheless, we remained the Three Musketeers, doing everything together. Living in a dog-friendly city provided many opportunities for dogs and pet parents to get involved in the community. One of our favorites was the annual pet parade. One year we dressed as medieval characters. I was a queen dressed in a historically accurate gown, Zoe was a princess, and Zorro a dragon. The BBC was present and adored our theme. They interviewed us. They told me afterward that they had never seen anything like this parade, and it was well worth their trip. A person actually approached me about a year later and said they had seen me with my dogs on the BBC news.

The three of us were all about the red carpet. One year we dressed as *Pirates of the Caribbean* characters, and they rode on top of their stroller, which was decorated as a pirate ship. As I made the turn onto the red carpet where the judges and cameras were, the stroller wheel caught on a wire and lurched. Zoe and Zorro lunged with it; Zoe falling off to the side. I caught her in my left arm, and she jumped right back up on top of the stroller, to the audience's amusement. They did a collective gasp, followed by a collective sigh of relief, followed by a collective cheer!

I knew that God had his guardian angels watching out for my fur babies, as they survived the seemingly unsurvivable. One day the gas on the stove was accidentally turned on when I reached for the microwave above the stove. I didn't realize that my body had leaned against the knobs and turned it on, but not enough to evoke a flame. The house was sealed up, as usual. I unknowingly had to work late that night and didn't come home for 12 hours. When I opened the door, I was overwhelmed with the smell of gas, to the point I thought I would pass out. Zoe and Zorro bolted toward the fresh breeze and me. I ran to open the windows and doors. I was so thankful that they were alive. Both were under ten pounds, and it was a one-story house with nowhere to hide. I obsessively check the oven knobs all these years later upon my departure since that day.

One night it was storming, pouring rain, with loud crashes of thunder, which is unusual for Long Beach. Earlier that day, Zorro went outside, chased a baby possum into the bushes, and wouldn't come out for hours, barking the whole time. We were all exhausted. We lay down to go to bed, huddling under the covers, trying to muffle the deafening sound of thunder. Zorro was terrified and shook like a leaf. The central heating system was on full blast.

All of a sudden, between thunderclaps, I heard what sounded like a cat screeching, followed clearly by a fur fight. The fur on my dog's backs stood straight up, and they looked at me, alarmed. Then it hit us. A skunk and possum had gotten into our attic heating system. The skunk had won, and spray came through every vent in the house, escorted by the full force of the hot air.

Zoe and Zorro were overwhelmed and covered with the odor. It covered my toothbrush and all that I owned. I smelled as if I were a chronic pot smoker at work for months. My high school students grew closer to me, as my colleagues were repelled by me. I had to lead a faculty development training for bigwigs in the district the next day, reeking of skunk. It was in my hair, all of my clothes, and it made me physically ill for days. I had to go around repeating the harrowing events of the previous night to explain my odor so I didn't lose my job and my credentials. I had all of the critters (possum family) and skunk humanely removed and relocated right away, but their memory stayed with us for a long time.

The three of us continued to enjoy life on day trips to dog parks, dog beaches, and dog cafes. We couldn't really enjoy dog parks, as many did not have small dog areas at that time, and I had been warned that a German shepherd had attacked and killed a Chihuahua at a dog park recently. The number of owners that did not properly supervise their dogs at the parks disappointed me. They were too busy socializing or on their phones to be aware of what their dog was doing.

Many people who are homeless took their dogs to the parks, and many of their dogs were not tame or trained. There were dog walkers who took so many dogs that there was no way they could be properly supervised. It was much like taking a small child to a playground and not monitoring his behavior. A bigger dog attacked Zoe one day when she was lying at my feet, so that was the end of our dog park days. The same was true at the dog beach, so we decided to take up shopping. Zoe and Zorro were lapdogs, not outdoor dogs anyway.

We loved car trips to San Diego. Zoe particularly loved going over

Coronado Bridge, so we made the day of it. I wanted a picture of Zoe and Zorro in their "I heart San Diego" shirts next to a famous dog statue in San Diego. It just so happened that it was in a plaza that was filled with individuals who are homeless and their large dogs. I was not deterred. I put them in their pet stroller, parked it next to the statue, and got the shot. Zoe's shirt a little too big, Zorro's a little too small, but still worth it; the homeless residents stared at me as if they were on a bad drug trip. They were speechless. It was getting dark, so I headed out as fast as I got in.

We traveled all over and did photo shoots of wherever we landed. We always headed straight for the local dog stores and boutiques. People often stopped to watch and smile along with us. They always rode harnessed in a dog seat in the backseat. One day I was particularly stressed and I rear-ended a car; the car seats saved their lives. It upsets me so to see people ride around with dogs on their laps, or free in the car; this causes so many preventable accidents and deaths. I have even seen little dogs fall out of the car windows.

We went to Downtown Disney, where they got Mickey and Minnie ears and shirts, and had a photo shoot outside the happiest place on earth.

Fourth of July was always a time of bonding, as we would huddle in the house trying to drown out people's illegal fireworks that were going off all around us. Roman candles and the like fill the sky all night long. I cannot believe that people believe it is okay to shoot off guns and illegal fireworks with no regard for animals or traumatized veterans.

One summer we visited my then-boyfriend's house for a barbecue. I wanted to impress him, as he wasn't particularly a dog lover; he had no experience with them. I was going to show him how well behaved my dogs were, so he would be sure to love them. Zoe enjoyed her carne asada, and Zorro made his way to the rose bushes to explore the new sights and smells. I looked up, as birds started to descend from everywhere, squawking. Zorro was eating a baby bird! I almost threw up. I started screaming. The fate of the bird was sealed. I was horrified and disgusted, as was Zoe. Zorro looked at me as if to say, "What?! It tastes like chicken." In spite of this first impression, when Zoe and Zorro were six, the boyfriend and I got married. They loved their new paw parent.

For Halloween one year, Zoe and Zorro dressed as tacos, and we dressed as taco truck drivers. We had a photo shoot in front of the local taco truck.

Christmas brought toys, treats, beds, blankets, and clothes galore—even their own treat-filled Advent calendars and stockings. Of course, a visit to Santa at the local pet store. We took annual Christmas family photos together. One year Zoe stood up on her back two legs and pushed Zorro in a sled for a photo. Another year they wore their favorite outfits; Zoe was in a beautiful Mexican dress, and Zorro dressed as the Old California hero Zorro, complete with cape, mask, and guitar. Our card read, "Feliz Navidad from Zoe and Zorro." The secretaries at work put it on display with my coworkers' pictures of their children on their Christmas cards. Zoe and Zorro were a hit.

Easter was filled with baskets brimming with treats, and a visit to the Bunny.

Birthdays were extra special, especially theirs. Zorro's was on Mexican Independence Day (September 16). I had special cakes made for them, and we would go out to eat. I bought them baby blankets with dog prints made especially for them from a couple at the county fair annually. They had their own dog-shaped ice cubes for their water bowls.

For Mother's Day, they got creative and did fur paw painting—much like finger painting that was printed onto shirts, cups, wall hangings etc. I would read them picture books about dogs, as they would listen and watch attentively. They would have nothing to do with the television. They wouldn't even watch the Puppy Bowl.

We attended "drive up church" services, where they would sit in the car with me and listen to the radio outside the church building, dressed, of course, in their Sunday best with crosses on their collars.

We also attended drive-in movies. We did 5k walks where I pushed them in the stroller. They had breast cancer shirts: "Doggonit, find a cure!" We strolled along beach paths. We stayed at local dog friendly hotels. This was a time when Chihuahuas and small dogs were very much in vogue, thanks to Paris Hilton, the *Beverly Hills Chihuahua* movie, the *Legally Blonde* movie, and the Taco Bell Chihuahua.

There were little dogcart boutiques everywhere, and Target carried aisle upon aisle of small dog clothes and toys. It was a good time to be a small fur baby. We drove through dog-friendly establishments for dog treats, such as "puppuccinos," "puppy patties," and "pup cakes." They loved to frequent Lazy Dog, In N'Out, Starbucks, and Wendy's.

I hosted Super Bowl/Puppy Bowl parties, complete with football-shaped treats, cheerleading outfits, and football toys. Zoe and Zorro got temporary tattoos at "Woofstock" in Northern California.

We went to a swap meet, where I concealed them in their pet stroller, covered by a blanket. A little boy walked by, and he was short so he could see into the little screened space where the dogs could look out. He saw them dressed and enjoying the ride. He turned to his brother and said in Spanish, "*Perros!*" (Dogs!). His brother looked at the stroller, assumed there was a baby in there, and said, "No, shhh! *Bebe!*" The older boy looked at me, horrified, thinking I would be offended and then relieved to see that I didn't look like I understood Spanish.

The little boy said again, "No, *perros!*" The older brother admonished him again and grabbed his hand to lead him away. I leaned over to the little boy and said, "*Si, perros.*" To which he gave me a big grin.

Zoe and Zorro made people smile wherever they went. Wherever we would go, people would say, "Aww . . . cute puppies." People usually referred to them as puppies, even when they were grandma and grandpa dogs. They were so small and still looked like they were young.

They loved sports. We went to a professional soccer game, where they sat up front, and the video crew spent more time taping them than the game. Zoe was dressed as a "Rufferee" in a black-and-white-striped shirt, complete with whistle around her neck, and Zorro was dressed in a soccer jersey with a soccer ball.

We also had our own Bark Box at Petco Park. We became Padres fans for the night. They were dressed in Padres gear and enjoyed receiving their Padres baseball toys and treats. The hot dogs were a favorite.

We celebrated every holiday in style. Zoe and Zorro enjoyed going to the groomer and getting their nails done and dressing up in theme. They had sombreros, Fourth of July sunglasses, Irish leprechaun hats, Valentine's Day outfits, Cinco de Mayo sombreros, and snow hats. At home when I bathed them, they had spa robes and their own rubber duckies. Whatever toy, treat, blanket, bed, and clothes one had, the other had to have it as well. I didn't expect them to share. I had never had a sibling, but I felt strongly that they should be treated equally. Equally spoiled, but not rotten.

We donned our life jackets and rode on a harbor cruise. Zoe was especially enamored with the sea and going under our local Rainbow Bridge in the Harbor that shares its name. She just loved bridges in general. She, of course, had to go on Rainbow Harbor Bridge as well, to get a bird's eye view of the city. Bridges bring people together, and that is just what Zoe did. She won fans wherever we went.

We were not without drama, however, on a regular basis. One time we had an earthquake that was high on the Richter scale. Zoe ran toward me, and Zorro ran from me. I ran for Zorro, scooped him up, and headed for the bedroom doorway where we shook up and down and looked at each other doe eyed. I was glad for their company in that moment . . . as in every moment.

One day, we were suddenly awoken by the howling of a dog a few houses down. Apparently his owner had backed over him with his truck and then pulled forward and ran over him again. The dog howled in terrible pain. It was so hard to hear. My dogs shook and looked at me like, "Are we next?" It was traumatic for us all.

We got a new neighbor who had a huge German shepherd that I privately named Cujo. He was so ferocious, and his "pawrents" were never home. He would throw his whole body against our fence, bark, and bare his teeth in the space between the fence posts at Zoe. She had no fear. She would stand right up next to his teeth and bark, defending her turf. This was a daily ritual.

One day when Zoe was almost 13, at a family outing, she looked up at me with an expression on her face that was filled with concern. I felt a still, small voice inside me say, "This will be Zoe's last healthy outing." I had no reason to think this, as we were having a great time, and she was so healthy and spry. I expected both of my dogs to live until 20 years of age, which was a possibility for dogs their size. She was only 12. Her eyes relayed the message; she was worried about something.

Soon after, when she went out back to urinate, she crouched for an unusual amount of time. I took her to the vet, and tests were run. Inconclusive, but probably bladder cancer. Only six to eight months to live. The vet gave me medicine to give her daily, to help ease her pain. I left the vet's office in shock.

I read all I could about canine cancer and what to do if your dog's time is limited, and we did it all. We had professional photos taken right away, while she was still feeling relatively good.

We celebrated her 13th birthday in style, complete with a special-order dog cake. I spent quality time with her, talking through memories of the many photo albums I had created of her life. I gave her the best brisket I had ever eaten in my life, and I could tell she agreed.

My dad died not long afterward, and I had to make the journey to Northern California to take care of his unfinished business. I realized that Zoe and Zorro had never been on a big trip before, so we decided to make it a bucket list family road trip. Zoe loved the adventure. She would hang her head out the window, the wind blowing her ears, as we crossed the Bay and Golden Gate Bridges, taking it all in, smelling the new smells, and seeing the new sights.

She attended my dad's memorial, dressed in her finest dress and necklace in her stroller, surrounded by the mystified homeless individuals who knew my dad from the streets.

She went to his ash scattering in the redwoods. I found joy in her as she looked around at the mighty giants and was so content to be alive. She made the whole grieving process bearable. The wind gusted through her fur at Trinidad Bay Lighthouse. She posed next to the White Fang wolfdog statue in Jack London Square. She wore her sailor dress at the Navy Sailor statue by the Golden Gate Bridge.

In the last months of her life, she had to wear diapers due to continual bleeding and urination. She looked adorable in her fancy diaper covers with pearls around her neck; after all, she still had her dignity. I took her into a single stall baby changing station to get her cleaned up before the next activity and photo shoot. Through it all Zoe smiled and loved her spirit-filled, abundant life.

She couldn't sleep with me anymore, especially in hotel rooms due to her bladder issues. She snuck onto the bed and looked at me coyly. I said, "Zoe, no dogs on the bed." And she looked at me like, "Zorro is your dog; I am your daughter." I pulled up a chair, and placed her bed on it; she fell asleep with my hand on her back. I missed our cuddle time together in bed. At home, she and Zorro now slept in bunk beds. He enjoyed the man cave feeling on the bottom, and she loved to be within an arm's reach of me, keeping an eye on my every move.

On our way home, we stopped in Solvang for a dog boutique. They had an area where there were actual dog-sized dressing rooms for your pup to try on elegant dresses and suits. I went in expecting to spend a fortune. The dressing room was Zoe's favorite pink. I chose a dress, and she looked at me as if she just didn't have the energy to raise her paws to put it on. I knew then that the end was drawing near, as she couldn't participate in her favorite activity, shopping. We left with empty hands and empty hearts. We took a picture at the statue in the park. She laid her head against mine as if to say, "It's time for me to go home, Mom." Therefore, we did.

I thought about anything else that was on the bucket list and remembered that there was a statue of a coyote in Pasadena that I had always wanted to show Zoe and Zorro. We knew it was our last chance, and we had better act fast. No clothes for the outing—just a short car ride. It was interrupted by a well-meaning woman who said that Zoe looked just like her dog that had lived 22 years. I cringed inside, knowing that mine would not see her 14th birthday next month. I felt cheated of time. She rallied, and we got the photo. Our last family picture. I hugged her; she no longer smelled like Fritos—she smelled of death, a scent I knew well. Her last meal was her favorite fast food: Wendy's bacon, chicken, and cheeseburger.

I prayed for God's guidance regarding the timing of her death. I knew my husband had to return to work soon, and I didn't want to be alone. I was scared. I was afraid of how I would react. I had never considered euthanasia until a friend talked to me about the home experience she'd had with her dog; she knew it was right for her and felt I should consider it. I just really wanted God to take Zoe in His timing and in His way. I was still praying for a miracle, although she had stopped eating and growled at Zorro if he got anywhere near her. The medicine no longer helped her pain. She was only an empty shell of herself.

What would have been my dad's birthday was the next day, and I didn't want Zoe to have to share a day of remembrance with a man not deserving of the honor of sharing with her.

I asked my husband to make the call for the day after. We were so impressed with the service, yet I prayed that Zoe would not need it. I felt so guilty—I had just agreed to the execution of my fur baby. All of a sudden, she rallied somewhat, giving me hope. I felt like I had made a mistake and was going to cut her precious life short. As if I had short-changed her ability to live and God's ability to heal. I continued to pray for a miracle, as I had the last ten months.

I laid out her bed, favorite toys, and blanket, and prepared for the vet to arrive in the morning. I stayed up late, holding Zoe in my arms. I said, "Love you, night Zoe," for the last time. A nightly ritual I held so dear for almost 12 years.

I really wished that she and I could have a conversation together so I could explain to her what was going on. I wanted her to understand. It must be so hard for parents of sick/dying babies because you don't know what they are thinking.

We turned out the lights. Less than an hour later, I heard Zoe yelp and scamper up from her bed that was now on the floor due to her not being able to get up into her bunk bed. I ran to switch on the light. I ran to Zoe, and she looked up at me, her eyes fixed on mine. She collapsed so that her head was under the bed, and I could not see it. She convulsed. Zorro stayed asleep at her side, my hero husband next to mine. I said, "It's okay, Zoe; it is time to go see Jesus. I love you." My fur baby was gone, and my life would never be the same. I am so glad that I am the last person she saw before she died, even though she gave me a look of desperation to help her, and I couldn't. I didn't cry, as I was in shock and denial. She stopped shaking.

It was just after midnight. She had made it to the day after my dad's birthday, she would have her own special day of remembrance, and it was as if she had known my thoughts and hopes.

My husband picked her up and took her to the bed we had prepared for the morning procedure. I said a prayer of thanks for my husband, as I could have never done that deed. I couldn't look at Zoe in the face, even though her eyes were open. I also thanked God for the role Zoe had played in my life and for taking her before she would have been taken. I thanked Him that Zorro slept through it all, even though his paw could have touched her while she died.

It is said that having a dog will bless you with the happiest days of your life—and one of the worst days. I found this to be true. The next morning the vet arrived for the appointment. She was so loving and compassionate, she eased my pain. She gave me a copy of a poem that brought me comfort.

Rainbow Bridge

Just this side of Heaven is a place called Rainbow Bridge.

When an animal dies that has been especially close to someone here, that pet goes to Rainbow Bridge. There are meadows and hills for all of our special friends so they can run and play together. There is plenty of food, water, and sunshine, and our friends are warm and comfortable.

All the animals who had been ill and old are restored to health and vigor. Those who were hurt or maimed are made whole and strong again, just as we remember them in our dreams of days and times gone by. The animals are happy and content, except for one small thing; they each miss someone very special to them, who had to be left behind.

They all run and play together, but the day comes when one suddenly stops and looks into the distance. Her bright eyes are intent. Her body quivers. Suddenly she begins to run from the group flying over the green grass, her legs carrying her faster and faster.

You have been spotted, and when you and your special friend finally meet, you cling together in joyous reunion, never to be parted again.

The happy kisses rain upon your face; your hands again caress the beloved head, and you look once more into the trusting eyes of your pet, so long gone from your life, but never absent from your heart.

Then you cross Rainbow Bridge together . . .

This poem, although a theory, brought me peace. I know Jesus is preparing a room for me in heaven, and I pray that Zoe and Zorro are in it.

The vet trimmed fur from Zoe for me to save and made a paw print impression for me to keep. She gave me resources for pet bereavement and informed me of the exact location where her cremated ashes would be in the ocean. I framed Zoe's collar, and put her favorite reindeer toy on display. I created a memorial area in her honor. I went shopping and bought every Zoe-looking dog item I could find. There is nothing like retail therapy. I ate emotionally all weekend, guilt free.

Dr. Seuss once said, "Don't cry because it's over, smile because it happened." I recited this mantra repeatedly through tears for a very long time, although deep inside I had a peace that passed all understanding.

I have always loved how the word *dog* is a palindrome for *God*. I believe that having a dog in our life teaches us unconditional love, just as God has for us. Dogs are great at fulfilling their purpose of demonstrating God's unconditional love for us, which we might not otherwise be able to fathom. He loves us in spite of who we are, not because of who we are. Zoe loved me in spite of all of my many shortcomings. She forgave me when I made mistakes and was always happy to see me, even when I was not happy to see myself.

It is an amazing gift, really. We all age, slow down, get gray hair, and gain weight—even dogs. We are given the unique opportunity to see an animal through all stages of life. In a span of a lifetime, a person could develop relationships with numerous animals and watch them come in and out of this world. This process has taught me a lot about myself, who I am, and what kind of person I want to be. As my kitchen towel says, "I want to be the kind of person my dog thinks I am!"

Zoe and Zorro were my faithful companions. If it weren't for Zoe and Zorro being there for me, I couldn't have been there for others. They worked behind the scenes. I had more issues than I had tissues. Zoe and Zorro were my "therapy dogs," as I believe all dogs are. They didn't need certification or a vest to prove it; they were just naturals. Zoe was my rainbow reminder of God's promise to me to never leave me.

I am a strong proponent for removing the stigma of talking about pet bereavement. We expect our children and students to stay strong and go off to school, and they are oftentimes closest to their pets. I fully support pet bereavement personal days for people to take off work and school as mental health days to aid in the healing process. I was fortunate in terms of timing; I was off work.

The death of a pet means the loss of unconditional love, a best friend, and a provider of security and comfort. There is no reason to feel ashamed of grieving this major loss. The loss of Zoe created a sudden life change in my routine. I actually missed washing her wet beds daily and caring for her as I would a newborn baby. I especially felt the loss when I would come home, and she wouldn't be at the door waiting for me. For many years, Zoe gave me a sense of purpose in life, a reason to get up and go on. It was truly life altering when she died. I considered writing her an obituary! Society does not encourage us to publicly mourn the loss of a pet, as it does a human. We have no kindred spirits to turn to, as in the death of a person. I had to create my own ways to memorialize her so I could begin the healing process.

Over the days following Zoe's death, I used her professional photo to have a necklace made of her likeness, as well as a blanket, pillow, shirt, candles, and even socks! I just wanted to be surrounded by her image. I put up framed pictures of her all over the house. She was already all over my phone to share as soon as people showed their children's or grandkids' pictures; Zoe's picture would make an appearance, and people would love sharing their dog stories with me.

I donated the majority of her clothes, toys, and supplies to the local shelter. I donated money to her rescue agency in her memory. I sent a thank-you gift to her vet and groomer, complete with her picture. I made memorial scrapbooks and photo albums. I journaled daily.

Although there is a pet cemetery nearby, I created a memorial garden in the backyard, complete with a headstone that reads "Zoe 2003–2017, All Good Dogs Go to Heaven." We visited the pier near where her cremated remains were scattered. I did everything I would do for a human loss to help me process my grief.

As time went on, I grappled a lot with guilt over the times I had been away from her when I went to work, school, social events, travel, and even my honeymoon to Hawaii that was cut short to a long weekend so I wouldn't be away from the dogs very long, especially since Zoe had been ill.

One day a few weeks after Zoe died, I was cleaning under the bed and found her missing blanket, avocado toy, and a sock ball that she had not had the strength to deliver. I collapsed into a pool of tears, wondering if I would ever fully heal.

I'd had so much loss in my life, but never did I grieve the way I did for Zoe. I had never cried so hard in my life. It was as if all the pain and loss of the previous years culminated together into this moment. I felt like I had a minor case of Post-Traumatic Stress Disorder (PTSD), as I was traumatized by the end of her life. I had dreams and nightmares about her for months.

The days and weeks rolled on into months. In October, I took out the Halloween/Day of the Dead bin and found Zoe's costume, her angel wings. I was dismayed, as I couldn't find her halo. I continued my search and found a moment of reprieve from grieving when I found her halo tucked into Zorro's devil costume. It brought a smile to my face.

Zorro continued to be . . . Zorro. He barked when I put him out back while Zoe's body was being removed. He didn't seem fazed at all. It was as if he was really looking forward to a bachelor's life. It was almost hurtful for me to see.

The day after her death, we got into the car with Zorro to go for a ride, and all of a sudden Zorro perked up. He jumped up and looked at the empty car seat next to him. He looked at me in a panic. He stood up on his back legs, which I hadn't seen him do before, and he looked out the back window, and then looked at me. He was going "wild chi." I had never seen him like this before. He thought we had forgotten Zoe.

Did he think I just discarded her after all of these years? Did he think it was his fault? Did he think we would get rid of him as well? I talked to him to reassure him. He settled down. He had finally noticed that she was gone. He withdrew from me. He wouldn't let me pet or hold him for a very long time. I grappled with whether I had made the right decision by not having him see her dead. He went home and slept on the spot where she had died. He never had slept there before. It became his new favorite place.

The day after Zoe died, Zorro developed such a bad cough that it impeded his breathing. He had to be taken to the vet less than 24 hours after our losing Zoe. They ran tests and x-rays and couldn't determine the nature of the severe cough, which he has never been able to shake. We even got a second opinion. We left, determined to make the most of the time we had together.

Zorro's 14th birthday was a couple of weeks after Zoe passed away, and although I was in no mood for celebration Zorro and my husband helped me to rally. We took Zorro to the Huntington Beach Surf Dog competition. We watched large athletic dogs and their surfer owners wow the crowds. Zorro had the opportunity to sit on an inflatable surfboard surrounded by a model wave for his picture. The second we placed him on it, he wiped out, rolling down the inflatable scene, unscathed.

The next dog was the champion from Australia that I swear did a number of poses on the model surfboard likened to a cartoon character flexing his muscles after a big win. Maybe Zorro wasn't born to surf, or even pretend to surf, but I started to embrace the quality time with my only remaining fur child. A woman came up and asked for his picture, which had become a regular occurrence over his lifetime. He looked especially handsome in his Hawaiian shirt, sunglasses, hat, and foam surfboard.

Like Zoe, Zorro made people smile. I had Zoe five months before Zorro, so Zoe and I had that special quality bonding time of just us that Zorro and I had always lacked. I noticed I had a lot more photos of Zoe, much like a first child, so I set out on a mission to make memories and take more pictures with Zorro.

I realized that Zorro is my last connection to my past. He has been the constant through my life of chaos. My mom; best friend, Jean; daughter; and even Zoe, all touched him before I lost them. When I hug him, I feel like they are hugging me. Needless to say, he gets many hugs and kisses.

We had to go to Texas to see my daughter in the hospital. Zorro was not doing well healthwise—he was really slowing down—and I couldn't leave him behind, so we made it a family road trip so he could comfortably go with us. Zorro smiled for photos while he ate barbecue in his cowboy hat in Texas, posed with cactus in New Mexico donning his sombrero, and—my all-time favorite photo of him—wore his sunglasses overlooking the Grand Canyon.

When we got home, we celebrated his *quinceañero* (traditional fifteenth birthday party, historically a Mexican rite of passage for Latinas). He partied, complete with a birthday cake made of peanut butter and bacon, and he received many new gifts, including a Batman costume and a bed for Halloween. We have made the most of every day.

Christmas came quickly, and I felt the loss. I hung Zoe's stocking next to Zorro's. I prayed for reassurance from God that I would one day see Zoe again. I felt like I needed a sign to complete my healing process so I could move on. I hung the ornaments that reminded me of her from over the years. There was a box of ornaments that my deceased best friend, Jean, had given to me, one every Christmas. I hadn't opened it in years. I felt compelled to look through it, although the tree was already burdened by the decor.

There it was. At the bottom of the box I found an item I hadn't realized I had; I didn't remember it even existing. An ornament of an angel, walking in the clouds of heaven, with a brown dog that looked just like Zoe with a rainbow next to her. The dog had a look on her face like, "I am waiting for you, Mom, and we will cross Rainbow Bridge together." I burst into tears, as I knew this was the sign I had prayed for and forgotten about. Zoe was waiting for me at Rainbow Bridge. I found rest for my soul, knowing she had found rest for hers.

Lessons learned from Zoe and Zorro:
1. Be the person your dog thinks you are.
2. Don't cry because it's over; smile because it happened.
3. *Dog* and *God* are palindromes for a reason.
4. Live the spirit-filled, abundant "Zoe" life.
5. Forgive freely.
6. Be loyal.
7. Greet others with zeal.
8. Bark less, wag more.

6.
Chloe's Box

Attending a friend's daughter's birthday party on the day my daughter would have been 24 was sobering. As I watched a little girl open her birthday presents with glee, my mind flooded with memories of my own daughter's childhood. Pink dresses, American Girl dolls, Barbies, Disney Princesses, all traditional toys for girls. The scene reminded me that I had a baby box for my only child that I hadn't opened in over twenty years. It needs to be cleaned out, as the items are being damaged due to being stuffed into such a small space.

I never had a baby box, as my mom kept nothing of my childhood. Besides, I no longer have a little girl who will grow up into a woman who wants to share her baby box with her children and grandchildren. That little girl is gone and, in a sense, dead. The loss of a child is something no one wants to think about, and as a parent you don't expect it to happen in your own lifetime, especially in the way I lost mine. Although I am cleaning out this pink box, it will be replaced with a similar blue one, to place the items of my now son. One offspring, two genders, one soul. One heck of a journey.

The first item from the box is a pink dress from her first birthday.

It looked beautiful on her. It was handmade like a work of art. Gold and fuchsia music notes with famous composers' names were etched into the material. A pink, velvet collar line, with a pink and gold rose pin under the chin. This dress looked like it was made for royalty. My mom and I had dreams of her becoming a concert pianist due to those long fingers she was gifted with.

My mom dreamed of her becoming the first female president, and I dreamed of seeing her name in lights as a contemporary Christian singer. My mom was living with me at the time, as neither of us had any money, and we had just moved to a new area. We didn't have money for either of us to eat, but we both knew she had to have that dress for her birthday, and we wanted to have our photo taken together with her in it. We both had new jobs, so we saved our money and made our first dream for her come true.

I entered the photo of my daughter in the JCPenney Cutest Baby Photo contest, and she won. Although the employee didn't know how to spell "Cutest," so my daughter became the "Cutiest." Any way you look at it, it was money well spent, as I showed off my misspelled certificate with pride.

My daughter loved to wear dresses and hats of all kinds. When she was in middle school, she chose her future wedding dress. It was a blue, tie-dyed sundress. Her dream was to marry our neighbor, who was in a Christian missionary family. His family eventually moved to Uganda, and my daughter had plans to one day move there with them and volunteer in the orphanages and schools that they built. She kept that dress after she grew out of it to use as a model for when she was ready to have one made for her wedding.

Our neighbor was smitten with her, as were many boys, and she was likewise crushing over them, absolutely obsessed with boys. Over the years, they became like family, as I would adopt them as sons and take them along on our outings. I don't know how she did it, but the boys were enamored with her. She prided herself on giving her mom advice about how to attract the attention of males. "Mom, no one wants to go out with a woman who has Chihuahuas all over her socks and jacket." Turns out, she was right.

Little did she know, but even before she was born I was praying for her future husband. Not only that, but also every aspect of her physical and spiritual self that I could think of. I guess I forgot to pray for her mental health and that she would feel comfortable in her own skin. I was 25 when I had her, so those weren't really things that ever came onto my radar. I was focused more on hoping she would have ten fingers and toes, not on if she wanted to have her nails painted. Gender dysphoria wasn't on my radar.

The next items in her box are her photo albums and scrapbooks I created over the years. I prided myself on being a "scrapper." I created hundreds of albums; they continue to be my treasures. Her baby album depicts her very first photo, taken by the nurse immediately after she was born. She has both arms up, with fists in a boxing pose. The nurse tried and tried to get the bald baby to put her arms down, or at least move them to the side; she refused, and put them back up like the cowardly lion that just found his courage.

I wasn't surprised, as being pregnant with her made me vomit at least once every thirty minutes for nine months straight. It was going to be an uphill battle all the way. This proved to be true from the start. She screamed nonstop with colic for six months. I couldn't wait to get back to work six weeks after she was born; I needed to get some rest. From the age of two, it was just the two of us, exactly as it had been for my mom and me. We were even 25 years apart, just like my mom and me. The cycle of divorce not only repeated itself, but at the same time in each of our lives.

As for the future, I should have had a clue when she was five. We had gone to Sizzler for our Friday weekly dinner. They gave us each a red and white circular mint on the tip plate. Chloe grabbed hers and began to unwrap it. I don't know why, but I always had a fear of her choking, so I had only one rule in my house: no gum chewing or small candy consuming for this reason. I said, "Don't eat that; it is a choking hazard. It is the perfect size to block your airway, and you just had ice cream; put it back." Chloe was so smart; I knew it was always better to appeal to her head and explain my requests.

I got in the car, and she piled into the back seat. I asked her how her day had been at school . . . no response. I turned around as I was backing the car out of the parking spot and found her holding her neck with two hands in the choking position; her face was purple, and her lips were blue. I screamed, "Oh God! Help me, Jesus!"

I slammed on the brake so hard it made the car lurch forward in a sharp, swift motion. I unbuckled my seat belt and ran around the back of the car to get her out and begin the Heimlich maneuver. She looked at me in shock. The hard candy had expelled itself when the car shook. Her color returned to normal, and she went on telling me about her day at school.

This was Chloe. No matter how much I tried to guide, counsel, teach, or train, she was going to do things her way, in her timing, to the beat of her own drummer; she had no interest in learning from my mistakes, or anyone's, for that matter. She was going to live life her way. For her whole life, she has always charged at death and leaned into danger and destruction. I was so grateful that God saved her that day that I made a vow to embrace every moment with her. She had to be the most photographed child on the planet. I made memories and took pictures to prove them. I have just gotten to a place where I can look at those pictures again, as for quite some time they evoked pain, causing me to relive my loss.

Chloe and I were so different even from the beginning. I was a right-handed, type A, organized, rule following, overachieving, hard-working, feminine woman. She was not. Yet our love for each other was deep and special. We enjoyed so much life together in her childhood. My albums were filled with smiles during mother/daughter bonding activities, such as traveling to Australia to pet a koala, to France to stand on the Eiffel Tower on Bastille Day, or making the guard laugh at Buckingham Palace in London with her favorite early childhood joke: "How much does it cost for a pirate to get his ears pierced? A buccaneer!"

I have albums of us having the Queen's Tea in Victoria, Canada; having her hair braided in the Bahamas; playing on the beach at Disney's private island, Castaway Cay; cruising to Mexico; riding in a horse-drawn carriage in Georgia; watching Fourth of July fireworks at Epcot Center; visiting the Little House on the Prairie museum and Mall of America in Minnesota; drinking out of coconuts and pineapples in Hawaii; shopping at the American Girl store in Chicago; meeting a Rockette in New York; viewing the skyline from the Space Needle in Seattle; petting the sea life at the aquarium in Monterey; making good use of our annual passes to SeaWorld, Adventure City, Disneyland, Knott's and Soak City; and shopping and dining all over Los Angeles, Orange, and San Diego counties, as well as all up and down the California coastline.

I have albums of when we were active in church, where she starred in many plays and musicals, some of which I directed. Photo albums of her playing the French horn, and the many parties I hosted for her friends. Of course, there are the typical photo albums of birthday parties with pony rides down the city streets, live monkeys in the front yard eating M&M'S, and the list goes on. All treasures of a life well lived.

I worked one full-time job as a professional school counselor and three part-time teaching jobs so that we could go anywhere and do anything we wanted to, especially in the summers when I was off work. Even though I had no assistance supporting her, she was going to have the life experiences that were never afforded to me.

I don't regret one moment or dime spent with or on her. As a child, she brought so much joy into my life and into my mom's life. They were very close. Over the years, my relationship with my daughter changed from a perfect ten to a zero, . . . back now to a seven. As we strive to return to our state of perfection, we continue to learn and grow through the seasons of life.

In a typical family structure, you could see the natural ebb and flow of a mother/daughter relationship. Like our lives, our relationship has been polarized by sudden extremes. We are ones who do not live our lives on the proverbial side of the mountain. We flourish in the valleys and peaks; meadows in between have not really been a part of our life experience, especially when it comes to our relationship.

It is said that childbirth is like a plane ride. While in the air, you feel tortured. When you land, you completely forget all the pain you had to go through to reach your destination, and you would be willing to hop back on that plane and do it all again. I would rather stay home. To emphasize that point, I feel that parenting is like going on a trip, but when your child is outside the norm it is a completely different experience.

Inspired by my reflection on Emily Perl Kingsley's essay "Welcome to Holland," I realized that, like many moms, I had envisioned parenting as paradise, much like going to Hawaii. I bought a bunch of guidebooks to make sure I experienced it all and didn't make any mistakes. I made all kinds of exciting plans and envisioned how this journey was all going to play out. I planned my wardrobe and photo ops. After nine months of preparation and buildup, I arrived at my destination. The pilot announced, "Welcome to Haiti!"

Huh?! Haiti?! They are known for secrets they keep from themselves! They are known for tarantulas! They have hurricanes and earthquakes! They have political corruption, poverty, debt, crime, and violence! This is a catastrophe! I have been planning on Hawaii! My dream is to go to Hawaii! I want to be taken to Hawaii! I demanded in denial. Nonetheless, I had been taken to Haiti, against my will, and there was no turning back. Not then, not ever. Hawaii was out of the question, I had to get used to Haiti.

I had to start over, buy new maps, read different pamphlets, and get a new game plan. I had to meet new people and learn a new culture, customs, and language.

With time, I realized that Haiti has some beautiful beaches and mountains and delicious coffee. It also has inspirational and resilient people, and I learned so much from this most unexpected of experiences.

However, I kept receiving pictures and postcards from all of my friends and relatives who were having the time of their lives in Hawaii, and "wishing you were here." Yes, I wished I were there too, but I wasn't, and I will never be. The grief that overcame me cannot be spoken because of that reality. There is a very significant and constant pain from the loss of not having a "typical child" that goes on and on.

Yet I learned that if I spend my life in self-pity that I didn't get to go to Hawaii, I can never be truly free to fully experience all that Haiti has to offer, and I will never understand God's purpose behind why I was there in the first place. I began to realize that there were some special things about Haiti that those in Hawaii would never get to experience, and for that I had gratitude.

When a loved one dies, grieving is difficult, although expected and accepted eventually. There is no such standard for a loss like the one I experienced, as there is no road map. I am a person who typically embraces change, new ideas, and adventure, but this time I found myself wanting the status quo and digging in my heels, refusing to move. Due to living in constant chaos that has been outside my control throughout my life, I place a high value on retaining control of what I can.

Through my grieving process over my daughter, I had to really learn how to give her over to God and let Him take control. I had to constantly remind myself that He loves her even more than I do, and He has her in His hands, if I will only open mine and give her to Him. Although I was very disappointed that she converted to Judaism, leaving her Christian roots behind, I am grateful that she still seeks God in her own way.

In my role as a professional school counselor, I specialized in working with students with special needs in various forms, and their families—including those who had lost their children to illness, accident, murder, or suicide. I will never forget a middle school girl with a very noticeable disability. My daughter befriended her in the Best Buddies after school program that I led. We took her with us everywhere. The stares were piercing. One thing that was unique about her was that she lived with her grandmother. Mom had a new boyfriend who looked like a Ken doll, and that wasn't surprising, as her mom looked like a supermodel straight off the pages of *Vogue*. Her daughter had major facial and bodily physical deformities. Her mom had every reason to expect paradise, even to get there in first class, but she landed in Haiti, where she made her daughter and mother stay while she escaped to enjoy another island.

One day at the fair, my daughter and I were walking behind a boy with Down syndrome who was erratically bouncing a basketball in a very crowded venue. He was hitting everyone hard with the ball. I thought to myself, *Where are this boy's parents?* As a teacher of students with Down syndrome at the time, I was concerned he was on his own, and my daughter and I decided to follow him to make sure he was safe.

The crowd kept giving me nasty looks and making comments under their breath about me not being able to control my child with that ball. I felt like holding up a big sign that read, "He is not my child." He wouldn't respond to me. My daughter always had a knack for helping children, especially those with special needs, and she caught up with him and asked him to play catch with her, to which he was happy to oblige. I ran over to a security booth and asked them to come assist. They directed me to the Lost and Found trailer, where the worried parents were waiting. My daughter encouraged him to follow her with the ball, and he made it back safely to his parents' arms.

I have worked with many parents whose children were incarcerated and in gangs. Loving parents who never expected their child to drag them to Haiti when they were Hawaii-bound.

There were my friends from church, a wonderful couple. Their son was born with a heart defect and had to have a transplant. They waited, agonizing over praying for a heart for their son, knowing that it meant that another family's child would have to die to donate a match. They were fortunate in that one became available just in time, and the surgery was so successful. Months after the surgery that was deemed a success, they found their son dead in his crib because of complications from the heart transplant. This couple had such courage as they held on through their crash landing.

Another lovely, wealthy couple were professional musicians. They had dreamed of their daughter following their example. She was born with cerebral palsy. She had every intervention and support known to man and made nothing short of miraculous strides. With all the money and social capital in the world, however, they never made it out of their unforeseen destination.

There are those who run away like my student with emotional disturbance who was never to be seen again in spite of all the posters put up around town. His parents never expected to spend the rest of their lives wondering if their teenaged son was alive or dead.

Much like a child who is kidnapped, who becomes a face on a milk carton, the back of a semi truck, or featured in the "Have you seen me?" ads on the back of promotional fliers in the mailbox, these children are in essence dead to the parent. They are lost, many never to be recovered.

Kidnapped, runaway, incarcerated long term, terminally ill, severely disabled . . . the parents are grieving the loss of their paradise, with the realization of their daily living hell.

The student who stands out the most to me was a sixth grader who was born as a female and preferred to be regarded as a male. She was my first transgender student. She was a forerunner in this area. She asked me for permission to use the male restrooms and locker rooms at school. We lacked an official policy at that time, so we agreed on the nurses' restroom in the interim. She was Mexican-American and had a large-statured dad who was a truck driver. He was a single parent who had recently moved here from Mexico.

At dad's insistence, the student kept her feminine name, although she wouldn't respond to it when attendance was called. She had been marked absent, although physically present, for weeks at the beginning of the school year. My student had mental health issues as well. She was obsessed with a girl at her previous school, and she would sleep on her front lawn and lie in wait for her all night.

That student's parents got a restraining order against her, and she was transferred to our school. I asked her why she felt the need to become a male, and she responded, "I am not comfortable in my own skin." This statement really saddened me, and on one level I could relate to it. I struggled with feeling comfortable in my own skin because I felt like I was a thin person trapped in a fat body. I was able to get her a therapist who specialized in working with LGBTQ teens, and she was grateful. I met with her dad, and I felt pity for him, as he lacked any understanding of what was going on with his daughter. He was in Haiti, and he didn't even realize it as he traveled for work all the time.

I also could relate to her dad, as my daughter was a student at my school, and she was 13 years old. When she hit adolescence, everything changed. She had moments in her childhood where she would act like a tomboy, want to wear boy's shoes, and play softball, but when she hit puberty her behavior seemed to be out of her control, almost as if she had a severe chemical imbalance. She was attending therapy and taking me on an emotional journey I didn't ask for or want to go on.

It was at age 16 that she started to wear a chest binder to prevent breast development. She started wanting to hang out more with masculine females instead of her typical male crowd. She didn't want to go for manicures, or shopping, or to put on makeup. She didn't brush her short hair or care about her physical appearance, as if this required too much effort to pull herself together. She was very defiant and disrespectful, well beyond that of a typical teen in a normal mother/daughter strained adolescent relationship.

She was exhibiting signs of extreme opposition. She was prone to anxiety attacks and developed numerous ticks. She became socially awkward and at times depressed. Although truly a brilliant mind, her academics suffered. Formerly a superb public speaker and singer, she spoke only in mumbles of deep tones that were inaudible and incoherent, as she intentionally lowered her voice to sound like a male. Even in the way she sat it was noticeable, and her table manners went from those of a queen to those of Oliver.

Her teen years were fraught with continual drama. She was not only gender nonconforming, but also nonconforming in so many areas of life. Refusing to wear the school uniform, self-mutilating by cutting and getting tattoos. She didn't just take the road less traveled; she wanted the road never traveled. She had five car accidents, resulting in one seriously injuring herself, and another the other driver. My daughter was doing everything within her power to develop into a man, and she did.

Although she never discussed anything with me, or informed me of her choices, when she was 18 she began taking male hormones, and her intentions were evident as she evolved into a person with male physical characteristics. At age 19, she had "top surgery" to remove her breasts. I learned about everything after the fact. Publicly, she presented as a male. I now had a transgender son. I was in Haiti, and it felt like Hades.

However, we both knew that our relationship had been a special and unique one in her childhood. We had experienced many challenges and losses together, and we had survived them with each other's help. We both valued each other's presence in our lives. To this end, we persevered in our attempts to have a relationship, so we decided to get lunch together. Riding a motorcycle, she showed up at my doorstep. I was going to follow her to our destination in my car.

I could barely look at her, as the testosterone hormones she had been taking over the years had made her hairline recede, and she was dressed in a white T-shirt with hair on her chest and arms, and blue jeans. Her face sported a full beard. The only part of her I now recognized were her brown eyes. I worried about what those prescription drugs were doing to her health. I knew what they were doing to her personality. The testosterone surge was making her more aggressive and impossible for me to communicate with, let alone live with.

She jumped on her bike and zoomed ahead of me quickly. I hated that bike, but at least she wore her black helmet. We would meet up, and we weren't going far. I saw her weaving in between cars ahead of me. She made the light that I, of course, stopped for. I heard a loud bang. The traffic in front of me slowed to a halt. *Where is she? What's going on up ahead?* I prayed for whomever was in the accident. As I ap-

159

proached, I could see the faces of the people lining both sides of the street. People were crying and panicking. There were no paramedics or police on the scene yet.

The cars continued to slowly go by the scene of the accident. I looked out my driver's side window, and there right below me was a person in a black helmet lying on the ground motionless. A car had hit the rider hard. The bike was in pieces all over the road. *Was it my daughter?!!* The person had on a white T-shirt, blue jeans, and a black helmet. The motorcycle was black, and she had been riding just in front of me. I gasped and prayed for help to calm down. Was it her?! The helmet face shield was up, but the eyes were closed. I could see the person clearly, but I couldn't identify her. I proceeded to the intersection near the scene to pull over where we were to meet up, and there was my daughter.

"What's wrong with you? You look like you saw a ghost, and you never cry; calm down!"

I was hysterical. I explained that I thought I had just seen her dead on the street, to which she responded, "Wow, you really do love me." She didn't even know the accident had happened. Turns out the young male driver later died. I left and went home and cried like a mother whose young daughter had suddenly been taken from her. My daughter was dead, never to return. Never would I hear her sweet voice on my voicemail again. Never again would I hold my daughter in my arms. All my dreams of having a best friend to shoe shop with, all the dreams of her growing up and wearing my pink wedding dress (or at least *a* dress!), all my dreams of having grandchildren who looked and acted like me . . . gone, gone to Haiti.

My loss, in contrast to those of others, was of a different nature. It is difficult in that the eyes don't change. No matter how altered the other physical characteristics are, the eyes are truly the window to the soul, and my daughter's eyes haunted me every time I looked at her.

How did this happen to my baby? In so many ways, these changes in her seemed to happen very suddenly and overnight to me. It all has become a blur, but I do know that at age 16 she left high school her junior year, eventually receiving her California High School Diploma Equivalency Certificate. I helped her set up her own apartment two separate times. I gave her two cars, one belonging to my mom and one to Jean. I remember her five car accidents and getting Jean's and my mom's cars restored for her more than once.

I got her scholarship money and set her up at the local community college in the honor's program, but she just had too many issues going on, and she was choosing to work almost full time and live independently, so she lost focus and dropped out. All of these choices were against my advisement, but she had other factors and people in her life that supported her in these endeavors.

Additionally, I had so much daily drama going on personally with the loss of my best friend to cancer, my mom to mental illness, my dad to homelessness, professional stressors, working multiple jobs, and going to school for my doctorate. At this point, there were just not enough tissues for my issues.

My daughter was forcing me to be on a turbulent plane ride, when life itself was already filled with trauma. I just wanted to get off and puke my guts out, but God helped me to hang on during my crash landing.

A common therapy technique that I taught my students was to write a letter to a person who has hurt you with the option of giving it to the intended recipient, tearing it up, keeping it, or whatever follow-up affords you peace of mind. I decided that it would behoove me to take my own advice, as she had moved to Boston to live in a community of people she felt were transgender friendly, where she disappeared and went off the grid for a period of time.

I was in the process of having a large tumor removed from my abdomen and on bed rest. I penned a letter to express my deepest hurts and frustrations regarding my loss. At the time, I wrote it largely for my own peace of mind, hoping that there would be an opportunity to share it in the future.

Dear Child of Mine,

I am writing this letter to let you know that I feel hurt by you. I am angry really, but as I tell my students, anger is often masked pain. I am in pain, and I need to release it somehow. You are "off the grid," and I can't contact you to speak with you directly, so this is my option. I want to start out by telling you that in spite of my pain, I do love you, but I really feel for us to be able to move forward in our relationship, I need to let you know how I am feeling.

I understand that you consider being a transgender person, not a choice you have made. That it is a medical condition in which your brain masculinized and your body did not causing strife and incongruence. You feel that the only effective treatment for your condition was a social and physical transition. Your body before lower surgery felt incomplete and you had dysphoria and shame. You pursued medical care to achieve the same normalcy and function that everyone else gets to be born with. Although on one level I disagree with you in that you have chosen to go through with your transformation decision, so I think we can just agree to disagree on that point and move forward.

With that said, I wanted to let you know how your transformation has affected me on a personal and professional level. I feel that you have been very self-absorbed during this process, and I want you to understand that it has a ripple effect and has adversely affected me in many ways you may have never considered.

Whereas I would never consider "outing" you to anyone, as it is not my business, I feel hurt that you chose to "out" me long before I was ready for that reality. I feel like you had no regard for my feelings in taking this action. When you took it upon yourself to contact our friends, family, and professional acquaintances to let them know about your transformation, I don't think you reflected on how that would affect me. Worse yet, you didn't even tell me that you had done this.

I wasn't ready to address their questions, lose some of their friendships and networking alliances, or graciously accept their expressed sympathy. At times, I felt like I was in the center of the water cooler gossip. I understand that being a transgendered person is more socially acceptable now then it was when you were younger, so perhaps some of the responses would be different now, but nonetheless, even considering our geographic location, at that time, it was not wholly accepted by some people.

I felt as if I went from having a scarlet DSM for being a Divorced Single Mom, to a neon green MTY for Mom of a Transgender Youth. I say neon green because although a little bit fashionable in some circles, it can also be a repellent, overwhelmingly bold, and unique like a cautionary tale.

I felt like you willingly and voluntarily became the poster child for transgender youth as you contributed to a book, and presented to the staff of our school with only a five-minute warning for me that you were doing so. I hadn't had time to process what was going on around me. I am sorry you felt like I disowned you that day, and I didn't want my peers to know you were my child. I was in a quick quandary I wasn't expecting. I spoke daily of the merits of my daughter with my coworkers, and I didn't know how to explain that the male they were watching was my daughter and you had begun transitioning while I worked there. I didn't think it was everyone's business to know our business. You didn't stop to take a breath and communicate with me. You did successful standing room only presentations at major universities and served as a mentor at the local LGBTQ center. All great for you as you found fame, but I still felt shame.

*I still had concerns about you physically and mentally. You met with me for dinner to inform me that you were going to DE-transition for a **second** time, you had changed your mind, and decided to go back to being a female, sent me pictures of yourself in a dress, and then changed your mind again, transitioned again, and decided to go back to being a male. This was all very confusing to me, and I needed time to process what you were feeling and doing, and how that would affect me. How could I expect others to understand if I did not?*

I felt like you were changing physically and mentally so quickly, that not all of your decisions were well thought out. You were raised as a non-denominational Christian and held very strong religious convictions, and yet you decided to convert to Judaism as a male. You previously had feminist views, and then decided to fulfill a very traditional male role in your marriage to a woman. You asked me to not "kill your son for murdering your daughter," and yet you were hospitalized twice for suicidal ideation, on top of almost jumping off a bridge and brandishing a kitchen knife at a police officer in hopes of being killed.

I understand when you said, "Realistically, my genetics are not the strongest in terms of mental health. I am not sure I would wish that on a kid; I really wouldn't want it to have a crippling disposition to just about every mental illness." I felt that was very mature of you, and I am so sorry that this is the way it is. What you didn't know is that when you texted me before your hysterectomy surgery, I was at a friend's "Grandma Shower" as she was going to be a first-time grandparent. I had to mourn the loss of fulfilling my dream of being a grandma someday while celebrating someone else's joy. This was not easy.

I know this journey has not been easy for you, and I am very sorry that you felt uncomfortable in your own skin. I am just asking that you slow down, and consider my feelings. I am sure you have many times, that I am not even aware, and I appreciate that.

You asked me to not leave you or abandon you when you told me, and I have not. Although I have felt abandoned at times like now as I try to recover from a major surgery. You also know that I don't agree with all of your decisions, and I constantly pray that you will make good choices.

Everything has happened too quickly. You marrying a woman you met on a hook up website not long after meeting, and moving to another state. The litany of surgeries without adequate time to heal.

I know I never shared my tears with you as I talked to you all those days in ICU. I hurt to see you hurt, and I was afraid I was going to lose you. You almost died because of your surgeries that some would consider optional or elective and have become possibly permanently disabled. It was so difficult to watch you suffer physically and emotionally with so much pain in the hospital and not to be able to stay with you since you were out of state. It saddened me to think that you had to go through all of that to feel whole, something I was blessed to feel since birth. God and I had many long conversations during that time. I trust that you had long talks with God during that time as well. Although you and I doubted it at the time, we were given hope for the future. More time for us to heal and grow.

In terms of where we go from here in the future, I am sorry if I have hurt you in any way, shape, or form, and ask for your forgiveness. I want you to know that I forgive you as well. Knowing that it is easy to forgive, and hard to forget, I still choose to love you unconditionally. I love you in spite of who you are, not because of who you are, and I hope you will afford me the same. I may not always agree with you, but I choose to extend grace and mercy into our relationship. Love is a choice, not a feeling, and in this situation, I choose love.

Please remember that I too am experiencing a traumatic transition, in terms of my understanding and mindset. Please be patient with me as I try my best to respect you by changing the name by which I call you and adjusting my pronouns. You know that I am not thrilled and delighted about this, but I am trying to be thoughtful and devoted as I am forced to integrate this situation into my worldview.

Thank you for reading this and allowing me to freely express myself. I am happy to discuss any of this further with you if you would like. I look forward to a day when I see you only as yourself.

Love always,
Mom

PS I hope you like the imprinted "Nice Jewish Boy" socks and Superman shirt and wallet I bought you for your birthday.

One benefit of having a transgender youth who is the poster child for his generation in my profession is that students who were aware of who he was started to flock to me for counseling. I felt honored that these young people entrusted my cisgender (non-trans) self with their challenging and often complicated lives. I had always enjoyed working with LGBTQ youth, but it was a different beast when it was my own child.

My son had many issues that warranted a series of diagnoses from various mental health professionals. It started off with anxiety and OCD (Obsessive Compulsive Disorder), followed by bi-polar, and then settling upon borderline personality disorder.

Although I was familiar now with mental illness, I wasn't as familiar with gender dysphoria. I decided to do some research and take a crash course to prepare myself personally and professionally. I learned a lot. It is not easy to be a transgender person, especially a youth. Studies have shown that they have a markedly higher suicidal ideation rate, as well as suicide rate, even outnumbering gay and lesbian teens. Studies have shown that as high as 41% of transgender people have attempted suicide.

When my son suffered from intrusive thoughts and suicidal ideation, we waited in the emergency room for hours, guarded by a police officer in case he opted to run. Fortunately, he was there on a voluntary basis that time. I was so proud of him for requesting the help he needed. He was finally assigned a bed at a psychiatric hospital two hours away from our house, although I visited him daily during his stay. It was such a sad and scary place. It made me reflect on all of the students over the years that I have had to hospitalize in my role as a professional school counselor due to suicidal ideation.

One year alone there were 22 that I referred to a psychologist for evaluation, all of whom were taken away in an ambulance due to being an imminent threat to themselves. In a caseload of 500, that was a high proportion. Now here I was on the other side of the desk, asking questions about insurance coverage. It made me a more compassionate counselor after that experience in working with suicidal students and their families. When he was let out of the hospital, they released him unannounced onto the streets two hours away from my home. He was taking a new medication that he had an allergic reaction to, and his throat started to swell closed while on the metro train trying to get back to a familiar area. He broke out into hives and itching and got sick to his stomach. He survived, but worse for the wear.

The second time he was hospitalized it was against his will, at the hand of his friend who was worried about his suicidal tendencies. The police took him away in handcuffs. His renter thought he had broken the law in the apartment, and he was almost evicted. At least he was hospitalized short-term locally, so visiting wasn't as difficult.

In spite of all of this, I am still grateful to his friend who sought help for him rather than watching him drown; she threw him a life preserver. Better to error on the side of caution. Still a hard place to go, and even harder to leave your loved one behind. It was evident to me that police officers need more training on how to engage people who are suffering from mental illness, suicidal individuals, and transgender people. Mental health workers need more professional development on how to help transgendered patients as well.

I understand now that Trans people can mourn their own selves. It is as if the person everyone thought was you is actually a close friend of yours; a Trans person has spent a lot of time being that person, and to know that that person is gone can evoke a grieving process. Transitioning alleviates a lot of mental stress for many people, but it is not without its challenges, including the physical, emotional, and mental processes. I am not the only one who lost my daughter; my child lost her as well.

Many aspects about being transgender are hard. It is harder for transgender youth to get a job. They face higher unemployment rates; financial challenges; lower average incomes; less social support; and stressors such as social stigma, rejection, stereotyping, isolation, victimization, discrimination, misinformation, and bullying, resulting in absence from school, which leads to higher dropout rates. They can suffer from lowered self-esteem, anxiety, depression, self-mutilation, and other mental health issues. Studies have also shown that there may even be a link between Trans identity and having been exposed to higher testosterone levels in utero; ear, hand, and brain differences; as well as higher rates of being lefties, lesbians, and people with autism.

I also learned that not everyone believes in marching with pride with regard to this issue. After all, there is no cerebral palsy pride march. Being Trans is a condition that a person may even feel afflicted or stricken with.

Some of my students identify as non-binary, neither male nor female, and prefer the pronoun "they." They are called the "tucutes" in urban slang. Those that are referred to as "truscum" (aka, transmedicalists) sometimes separately class themselves. Those individuals are what most would refer to now as transgender. There are a whole range of terms and expressions, including transtrenders, traps, imposters, fakes, transqueer, xenogender, . . . and the list goes on. There are those who have gender dysphoria and those who do not. They vary in philosophy and expression.

Many are victims of having been verbally abused, physically harassed, and sexually assaulted—even in some cases resulting in murder. They can have higher rates of Post-Traumatic Stress Disorder (PTSD) due to suffering from physical, sexual, and/or emotional abuse. Many are victims of Transphobia, Trans prejudice, and Trans bashing.

Many Trans youth suffer shame and drug use. They run away and are homeless. They can experience transgender oppression (having to deny their gender of the past.)

Knowing all this, who would want his/her child to have to go through this torture? Who would choose this for his/her child? I didn't. Life is hard enough without throwing all of these challenges on top of it. Yet it is not about what *I* would choose; it is not *my* life.

For my son, his gender expression changed in his teens, followed by what he refers to as a gender affirming procedure (top surgery). This procedure of removing his breasts had complications. This was followed by a hysterectomy, when he also experienced serious complications that landed him in an emergency room. Lastly, he had "bottom surgery." This is a major reconstructive surgery below the belt. He opted to have this surgery to mitigate his incongruent feelings regarding his body. He informed me that he felt like a "freak" stuck in between two genders, and he just wanted to feel "normal."

This resulted in ten major corrective surgeries in 12 months, with almost a month's stay in ICU, although he had the top surgical team in the country. Not to mention being transferred to a nursing home. Less than 1,000 surgeries of this type have been performed in the US, so the science is still in its infancy. In this case, it almost took my son's life. I am so angry that Hollywood and magazine covers do not accurately portray how very serious and difficult this surgery is—it may indeed end your life. Young people need to know the risks and count the costs before making these types of decisions.

However, this is no longer a matter of just teens experiencing these stages; children as young as preschool age are now expressing their gender earlier than ever. I still have so much to learn about this topic, and I feel as though I have already learned so much, but human behavior is a complex issue. I am very grateful for the lessons I have learned from my son along the way.

I had to go through a transformation in *my* time, in *my* way. I had to spend time praying, reflecting on my faith, and considering what God would have me do in this situation. Every person is on his/her own journey, and what is right for me may not be right for another. I chose to extend mercy and grace, which is what God has extended to me.

My son is now almost 25 years old. He has had numerous "bottom surgeries" and still suffers physically and mentally, but in some ways we are now connected more than we have been in years. I have started refilling his box. He co-authored a book about LGBTQ teens for schools, and that has made its way into the box. In addition, pictures of him presenting at major universities for LGBTQ youth and their families.

Although his box doesn't look like a pretty package with a bow, I can still hold my chin up. Not all is lost. He values education and is a gifted public speaker, a prolific writer, and an amazing intellectual, destined from my perspective for greatness. I look forward to one day reading his own book so his voice can be heard, as it is valuable.

I realize that there is my truth of my lived experiences with him and his truth of his lived experiences with me; the reality of our lives together is probably somewhere in the messy middle. I enjoy shopping for my daughter-in-law, and I love my ill-mannered grand dog and enjoy spoiling him even more rotten than he already is.

My son has faith, morals, and values, loves to celebrate life, and has some outstanding character traits. He is a hard worker and excellent at his job. He attends college and values education. Overall, he has assimilated many of the lessons and attributes that I had felt he rejected. At age 18, he legally changed his first, middle, and last names and used my name as his middle name to honor me and retain the meaning. I can now say that I have fared better than those who have lost their children to death. I can still hug my son and wish him a happy birthday, where they cannot.

I miss hearing his voice when we don't get a chance to Face Time, which I prefer over a voice call. I like to look into his eyes. I like comparing notes about our favorite reality television show. I like hearing about his day and sending him and his wife care packages. I like shopping for him and buying feminine looking jewelry for his wife. I look forward to us perhaps one day writing and presenting together. I look forward to him having dinner at our house, even if we don't eat the same food (but the rule remains the same: no gum chewing or small hard candies allowed!). He has a lot more choices to make in his life, many of which I am sure I will not agree with (did I mention he's a vegan!), but at least I will have him to hug on his birthday and not be visiting his gravesite following his suicide.

I continue to pray for him daily, and for me. We are not at a perfect ten yet on our relationship scale, but we are slowly but surely getting there. Some days one step backward before another two steps forward, but we are in motion.

Chloe's Box

It was time to finally go to Hawaii. My husband and I traveled there so I could present at an international conference on education with a researcher from Japan. My son created an amazing PowerPoint presentation for me to proudly use. I felt like I took a piece of my child with me to Oahu. Our relationship is now moving in the right direction. As my husband and I were waiting for the plane to take off toward home, and we were relishing in the glow of our dream vacation memories, he asked, "So where should we visit next year?" To which I responded, "Hmmm . . . you know, I hear there are nice beaches in Haiti."

Lessons learned from my child:
1. "Life is either a daring adventure, or nothing." (Helen Keller)
2. "I took the road less traveled, and that has made all the difference." (Robert Frost)
3. "Go confidently in the direction of your dreams, live the life you have imagined." (Henry David Thoreau)
4. "Why fit in when you were born to stand out!?" (Dr. Seuss)

7.

Living Legacy Box

Well, friend, there is only one box left, and you are sitting on it. You asked me earlier whose box it is, and you have hung in there with me for the duration of my other six boxes, so I will tell you.

The seventh, empty, box is mine. I know I am alive and well, but it is important to get prepared for when that day comes when I am not.

I know this sounds morbid; that is why I try to put a positive spin on it and call it a Living Legacy Box. I recently created my legacy box. I try to keep it to three items and only one box, as I have learned that it is hard to store more than that and could become burdensome to my loved ones after I am gone. My items represent the core of who I am, and the lessons and memories I want to impart upon my departure from this earth. I may change the items over time. It is similar to leaving a living will, but I am including tangible items as visual reminders to my loved ones. For now, my three items are:

1. My Bible

My Bible is old, highlighted, and torn, but it reflects who I am at the core of my being. I inherited my best friend, Jean's, Bible, as I had bestowed it upon her. I love to touch the tear-stained pages and reread the highlighted verses of faith and hope in her Bible.

I had a student with special needs once when I was a teacher. He didn't know his mother, as she was incarcerated for life. He carried her Bible everywhere he went. He would sniff and caress it. One day I asked him about it, and he said that it brought him comfort to know that she had held it in her hands; it was as if she were giving him a hug when he embraced it. For me, my Bible represents leaving a legacy of unwavering faith.

When I was a young child, my mom was my Sunday school teacher; she had a crush on the young, single pastor and invited him in to speak to our class at Christmastime. He told the story of being a young boy who wanted a board game for Christmas that he had pointed out to his parents. It was the size and shape of a small box. The gift sat under the Christmas tree all season, and he rejoiced over knowing in his heart that it was the game he had requested. It would be his only gift, but he didn't mind as it was exactly what he had asked for.

Christmas morning came, and he tore open the present to find . . . a Bible. He was so confused and shocked; it wasn't what he had hoped for at all, and even worse, it was something he had never wanted to ask for. His dad explained to him that the gift he received was the greatest gift possible, and it would keep on giving to him throughout his lifetime, long after his parents were gone. The young boy didn't really grasp this concept at the time, but over the years he continued to go to church with his family and read his Bible, and he indeed found it to be better than a board game in which he would have lost interest as he grew.

I was mesmerized by the story, and every time I think about it I am that first grader sitting on the old carpet, eating my stale animal crackers and drinking orange Tang in a Dixie cup listening to the pastor, wishing he were my dad.

I told my mom that day that I wanted a Bible now that I could read. She said I had to earn it by reciting the 23rd psalm in front of the congregation with the other students in the class. I am so glad that she helped me value the Bible and memorize Scripture. This is her greatest legacy left to me, and I desire to pass it on to others, as it has saved me figuratively and literally.

Through all of the losses I described, my Bible was the tool that kept me grounded. I leaned into it, wept into it, and was encouraged by it. The God who was the same yesterday, today, and forever still speaks to me through His Word and gives me peace for my soul. No physical item brings me greater peace than my small, black leather New King James, Thomas Nelson Bible that I have carried in my purse throughout my lifetime.

Some of my favorite verses are highlighted in numerous pastels with stars lining the margins. An example is Romans 8:28: "And we know that all things work together for good to those who love God, to those who are the called according to His purpose" (NKJV).

I have learned that God will not only bring me out of my crisis; he will bring me out better than I was before. I will not just survive—I will thrive. Retaining this mentality has helped lessen my stress, worry, and anxiety, and it has allowed me to relax and enjoy my life more fully. Faith, not my emotions, moves me forward. God is in control; even when plan A is crumbling at my feet, God has plan B awaiting in the wings. This is not a result of any action I have done or my love for God; it is due to God's love for me.

2. My diplomas

I received an excellent formal education by the grace of God. I was a "whiz by no means," as my mother so clearly put it to my dad in her letter, but I was a hard worker who understood the value of education, thanks to my mom's prompting. I do believe that education is the great equalizer, but I also acknowledge that not everyone is as privileged as I am. Some of the wisest people I have ever met have no formal education. Some of the most brilliantly educated people I know have no common sense whatsoever. My education made the difference between homelessness and prosperity for my mom, my daughter, and myself. To value hard work and education is a legacy that is worthy of our leaving.

My educational journey spanned decades and varied in terms of the quality of the schools and the education I received at them. Two elementary schools, one middle school, four high schools, one community college, and four universities, spanning two states, have led me to where I am today. Although I believe that education is the great equalizer, I fully acknowledge that schools are not equal in terms of facilities, quality of instruction, or resources. I have attended and been employed at some of the nation's best and some of the nation's worst. One thing I know rings true at them all: cream always rises to the top. Hard work and making the most of all opportunities given to improve oneself intellectually constitute a worthy endeavor that will be rewarded.

I have a doctorate in educational leadership, and I still don't know all of the answers to our nation's issues, but I do know that, on a personal level, my education has assisted me in my ability to cope with tragedy and loss. I have developed the academic resiliency skills of writing in my journal; reading the Bible; communicating with others; and other skills, such as researching resources to aid me in my healing (to help me process and cope with my loss). I believe that Albert Einstein was right when he stated, "The more I learn, the more I realize how much I don't know." Learning is a lifelong endeavor, and I continue to pursue it on my personal journey to excellence.

The academic knowledge I have gleaned over the years has afforded me upward mobility through socioeconomic classes that is a privilege not afforded by most. These experiences with diverse groups of all kinds have enabled me to easily assimilate to wherever God calls me to serve. These opportunities have exemplified for me that no matter how bad I may have it, there is always someone else who has it worse.

If I can't find someone in need in my backyard, I open my eyes to the world at large. Being a healthy, white, middle class American residing in Southern California makes me one of the most privileged and blessed people on the planet. Perspective is important, and I am exposed to others' lives through education, which reminds me that my lack is another's abundance. Sharing my knowledge formally and informally with others who have not had the opportunity to experience education as I have is a noble endeavor that I continually strive to achieve.

I once saw a commercial on TV (when I was deciding if I should leave K-12 public education and teach full time at a private university) about a nurse educator. The narrative said that this one woman saved hundreds of lives today without leaving her classroom. The video cut to many nurses helping all over the country in various settings, and you later find out that the woman had taught every one of them, and they had gone out to help and teach others.

That is when I decided it was time to affect a greater number of people by teaching others how to change lives through school counseling and school psychology. I am grateful to those who have taught me over the years. Teachers of all kinds and levels should be honored and respected, as teaching is one of the noblest professions. My diploma reminds me of that calling.

3. My writings

I believe that God is the creator, author, and sustainer of my life. He is not only the author of my life; He is also writing a story in my heart. He has used death and life, blessings and challenges to serve His purposes in my life. My personal testament of what God has done in my life is now intermeshed with the testimonies of those whom I have lost. I find joy in discovering whenever God takes my life, that is a hot mess, and creates a cool message for me to share.

The losses of Jean, my mom, my dad, Zoe, Paul, and Chloe have made me aware of what a life lived with God, especially in times of pain, can look like. Second Corinthians 3:2 reminds me that I am a letter written on hearts known and read by everyone. My lost loved ones have written love letters on my heart, and it is my desire to write letters on others' hearts of love and faith in spite of circumstances.

I love to write. I have scrapbooked and journaled since I was in elementary school. I have included some of my special journals in my box. When I was 27, I learned about miracle recording. It was then that I started a journal to record the amazing miracles God had done in my life—the answered prayers. I write the date and one sentence to remind me. I have been doing this for over twenty years, and my journal continues to develop all the time. When I need encouragement, I reread what God has done for me in the past, to help me remember I can trust Him with my future. My testimony is mine and mine alone, and I believe it is another legacy worth leaving.

Sometimes I journal for myself. Sometimes I journal for an intended audience, such as for my child. Sometimes I write letters to God. Sometimes I write about my joys and daily living activities, and sometimes I write about my sorrows, such as grieving. I have found this to be a very useful strategy to help me process what I am experiencing. Some people are able to participate in art therapy, a hobby, or physical exercise to relieve stress, but for me writing down my feelings helps me to understand them and let them go. I believe that everyone needs a coping strategy, and one that has been most successful for me is journaling. It helps me dissect the mess out of the message that I feel God is trying to impart to me.

Often I read a daily devotional or Bible passage and write about it. For many years, I read the One Year Bible in every version printed and made daily notes comparing and contrasting the translations. This went on for a good ten years.

I have expensive leather-bound journals; cheap spiral notebook journals; messy journals; neat journals; long journals; and short, unfinished journals. I have journals that have Bible verses imprinted on each page, and journals that have inspirational quotes on each page. I have journals with Bible verses on the cover, such as my life verse, and one of my favorites, Ecclesiastes 3:1–8

There is a time for everything,
　　and a season for every activity under the heavens:

　　a time to be born and a time to die,
　　a time to plant and a time to uproot,
　　a time to kill and a time to heal,
　　a time to tear down and a time to build,
　　a time to weep and time to laugh,
　　a time to mourn and a time to dance,
　　a time to scatter stones and a time to gather them,
　　a time to embrace and a time to refrain from embracing,
　　a time to search and a time to give up,
　　a time to keep and a time to throw away,
　　a time to tear and a time to mend,
　　a time to be silent and a time to speak,
　　a time to love and a time to hate,
　　a time for war and a time for peace.

I have journals that offer prompts that I respond to. I have lined journals, unlined journals (I am not a fan of those; I need guidelines). I have empty journals that were gifts or I just haven't gotten around to starting yet, but I liked them so they are waiting dutifully in line to be filled. No matter the cover, the content represents who I was at a given moment in time. I have journals with locks on them, although I prefer to not have locks, as I typically over the years lose the key. I live a transparent life anyway; I wouldn't panic if someone read them, but I would be disappointed if a fire consumed them.

I love reading back entries in my journals, as many times I don't remember anything about my tearful rants or pleading to be released from some burden that was so overwhelming at the time but is completely forgotten at present. I see my misspellings and poor grammar. I shake my head at my immaturity and foolishness, but I remind myself that this is how I can measure growth. I am not the same person I was, and I hope anyone who reads them one day will remember that. I am constantly changing into the Christian woman God intended me to be.

My writing is my proof to myself that I am growing; moving; and, most importantly, still living, surviving and thriving. I like to reflect on them and my life journey.

For the boxes I have organized today, I go through them usually once or twice a year. Typically, I do this on the anniversary of the person's death, or maybe even the person's birthday, or on a day I feel like I am particularly stricken with grief and need to feel close to that individual. Through all of the losses that I have shared with you, I have learned a lot about life, living, dying, and death. I also learned that my resiliency factor in life has been my faith. Relying on God and my faith in times of trouble has been my strategy that has served me well. Through these losses, God has truly given me, as Isaiah 61:13 says, "a crown of beauty instead of ashes, the oil of joy instead of mourning, and a garment of praise instead of a spirit of despair."

This is a lesson I have learned that I want to share with others. It made me think about what the artifacts would be in my legacy box. I want to be a blessing from generation to generation. I don't want my influence to end when I physically cease existing on Earth. God has woven together a beautiful story of my life through the people I have met and the challenges I have endured.

I know I was born for a purpose. I want to lead, teach, and inspire others to become the people God intended them to be. I want to leave an intentional legacy of living life through a filter of faith. This "faith filter" helps me to see, with God's eyes, my life as chapters of the past shaping who I am today. This faith filter has kept me from falling into the trap of a "fear filter." If I had not had so many excuses to succumb to fear, I wouldn't have had so many reasons to pursue faith.

I know I was born at this time, in this place, for this reason. It is by no coincidence that I invited you here today. I believe that it is a "God incidence," as you need some encouragement yourself.

My name means "Excellent worth, shining with fame." My life

verse is Philippians 4:13: "I can do all this through him who gives me strength." Knowing these things about myself has given me an inner fortitude to carry on in adversity.

My attitude of gratitude and eternal optimism have served me well along the way. In spite of it all, I know that God not only loves me—He likes me. I have attempted to embrace the unseen benefit in every scenario. This has helped me build a sort of spiritual resilience that allows me to carry on through adversity. I feel confident that God will use my story for His glory. I strive to seek God and put Him first in all things, personally and professionally.

Even though I did experience varying levels and forms of the stages of grief (denial, anger, bargaining, depression, acceptance), I tried to not dwell on them. I attempted to move forward to what I would consider a sixth stage, that of hope.

Well friend, I know this has been a lot to process, and I really appreciate your help. I have accomplished a lot today. That sound was the big metal hallway door slamming; time to go before the lights go out. I can't wait to find out what you put in your legacy box. It will be my chance to get to know you better. I hope you love leaving a living legacy, as I have.

I will walk out with you; may peace be with you, friend.

Lessons I have learned from life:
1. View my life through a filter of faith.
2. God not only loves me; He likes me.
3. Formal education is the great equalizer.
4. Strive to go beyond unconditional positive regard to unconditional love for others.
5. I was born for a purpose at this time, in this place.
6. Journaling helps me process this precious gift called life.

Study Guide

Jean's Box

FOLLOW UP QUESTIONS:

1. Who is your Jean? Who do you know whose life has been affected by cancer?
2. What can you learn from your Jean?
3. What can you do to help that person's legacy live on?
   Give your heart: Pray for those that are suffering from cancer, for their friends and families, the health professionals, and the researchers.
   Give your time: Walk in an awareness 5K; get a mammogram.
   Give your talent: Volunteer to help a person with cancer.
   Give your treasure: Donate to breast cancer research.

RESOURCES

- Susan G. Komen Foundation
- American Cancer Society
- Avon Three Day Walk
- Breast Cancer Angels
- Living Beyond Breast Cancer

Paul's Box

FOLLOW UP QUESTIONS:

1. Who is your Paul? What young person do you know that is your hero?
2. What did you learn from your Paul?
3. What can you do to help that person's legacy live on?

   Give your heart: Pray for children with life-threatening diseases such as cancer, pray for their friends and families, pray for the health care workers and researchers, and pray for a cure.

   Give your time: Join PTA; actively participate in your local school as a parent, business partner, or volunteer.

   Give your talent: Be a mentor to a child.

   Give your treasure: Donate money to a nonprofit charity; donate toys/school supplies to a local hospital, school, or youth organization; say yes when asked to round up or give your change or make a small donation at the store.

RESOURCES

- Best Buddies
- Special Olympics
- Ronald McDonald House
- Make a Wish Foundation
- St. Jude's Children's Hospital or a local pediatric hospital
- Lokai Bracelets

Maybeth's Box

FOLLOW UP QUESTIONS:

1. Who is your "Maybeth?" Who do you know whose life has been affected by domestic violence or mental illness?
2. What did you learn from your "Maybeth"?
3. What can you do to help that person's legacy live on?
   Give your heart:
   > Pray for those who are victims of domestic violence, their friends and family, and those agencies that assist them.
   > Pray for those who suffer from mental illness, their friends and family, and those who help them.

   Give your time: Volunteer your time to help a person who is a victim of domestic violence or suffers from mental illness.

   Give your talent: Volunteer at a women's shelter or nonprofit that benefits people with mental illness. Go to the doctor for an annual physical. Call the Domestic Violence hotline to get help. Walk in an awareness 5K.

   Give your treasure: Donate to a women's shelter or support center for those who suffer from mental illness.

RESOURCES

- Domestic Violence Support Hotline
- National Alliance of Mental Illness (NAMI)

Study Guide

Jack's Box

1. Who is your "Jack"? Who do you know whose life has been affected by alcoholism, drug addiction, or homelessness?
2. What can you learn from your "Jack"?
3. What can you do to help that person's legacy live on?

   Give your heart:

   > Pray for those that suffer from alcoholism, drug addiction, and/or homelessness.
   >
   > Pray for their friends and family, especially their children.
   >
   > Pray for those that work to assist them.

   Give your time: Volunteer at a homeless shelter, even beyond Thanksgiving and Christmas.

   Give your talent: Donate used clothing and articles to nonprofit organizations that assist the homeless. Raise awareness of the homeless in your community, advocate for social justice by giving them a voice, and vote when their well-being is at stake. Seek treatment for yourself or a loved one.

   Give your treasure: Donate to organizations that systematically assist the homeless and drug addicted in your community—no handouts, only hand ups.

RESOURCES

- Pets for the Homeless
- Alcoholics Anonymous

187

Zoe and Zorro's Box

FOLLOW UP QUESTIONS:

1. What pet is your "Zoe"? How has your life been affected by your relationship?
2. What can you learn from your pet?
3. What can you do to help other animals?

   Give your heart: Pray for animals that are abused, homeless, and in shelters.

   Give your time: Volunteer at a local shelter, be vocal, and support laws that take action against those convicted of animal abuse; support laws against illegal fireworks and leaving pets in cars.

   Give your talent: Be a responsible pet owner—adopt from a shelter, not a pet store or breeder; get your pet fixed, micro-chipped, immunized, and licensed; install a pet car seat in your car; supervise your dog at parks and beaches; keep pets indoors during firework season to lessen the load of runaways at rescue agencies; and don't leave your pet in the car, even for a minute! A window cracked open is not enough! Know your state's laws regarding freeing an animal locked in a car. Save a life: adopt a new fur baby today!

   Give your treasure: Donate to the ASPCA and local no-kill animal rescue agencies.

RESOURCES

- ASPCA and the Humane Society

Chloe's Box

FOLLOW UP QUESTIONS:

1. Who do you know that is LGBTQ or who has threatened, attempted, or committed suicide?
2. Who do you know whose life has been affected by a friend or family member who is a member of the LGBTQ community or who has threatened, attempted, or committed suicide?
3. What can you learn from them?
4. What can you do to support suicide prevention?

    Give your heart: Pray for those in the LGBTQ community and/or those whose lives have been affected by suicide.

    Give your time: Listen to a youth without judgment.

    Give your talent: Volunteer your time to help a suicide hotline or teen center, and extend a life raft.

    Give your treasure: Donate to a cause such as the Trevor Project (suicide prevention for the LGBTQ community) trevorproject.org or YellowRibbon.org (suicide prevention program).

RESOURCES

- The Trevor Project at trevorproject.org
- Yellow Ribbon Suicide Prevention Program at yellowribbon.org

Bobbi's Box

FOLLOW UP QUESTIONS:

In creating a legacy box, consider the following questions.

1. Who am I?
2. Where am I going?
3. How am I going to get there?
4. What physical items reflect favorably on my life's journey (pictures, journals, artwork, diploma, Bible, etc.)?
5. What have I learned in life that I want to teach others?
6. How has what I have learned changed me?
7. What message do I want to convey to others through artifacts?
8. What do I stand for? What is important to me (education, spirituality, giving, volunteering, etc.)?
9. What does your name mean? What is your life verse? (You can find this online or in a baby-naming book.)

Let's continue the conversation around removing the stigmas of those issues discussed in this book; look for *Seven Boxes: An Inspirational Memoir Celebrating the Strength to Move On* online and on social media platforms such as Instagram and Twitter.

Acknowledgments

First and foremost to Christ, through whom I can do all things.

My utmost gratitude to my husband, Aurelio, who is the answer to my prayers and an amazing editor!

Additionally, I have been blessed with the guidance and support of many. These include authors Dr. John Trent, Debra Ginsberg, Barbara Abercrombie, Donna Hilbert, Jonathan Alexander, and Ann Hamer for their input and wisdom.

Also Jean, Paul, Mom, Dad, Zoe and Zorro, and my child: Thank you for sharing your journey with me.

I am also indebted to Big Daddy Weave, whose song "My Story" motivated me.

Finally, to Tim Beals and the Credo House Publishers staff for helping my dream become a reality.

About the Author

DR. BOBBI ALBA is a professor at Azusa Pacific University in the School Counseling and School Psychology department. Previously, she was a teacher and professional school counselor in a K–12 setting. *Seven Boxes: An Inspirational Memoir* is her first book. She currently resides with her husband in Southern California. Follow her on Twitter @DrBobbi728 and Instagram dr.bobbi728.